The Brand Gym

The Brand Gym

**A Practical Workout for Boosting Brand
and Business**

David Taylor

JOHN WILEY & SONS, LTD

This publication is designed to provide accurate and authoritative information in regard to the subject
matter covered. It is sold on the understanding that the Publisher is not engaged in rendering
professional services. If professional advice or other expert assistance is required, the services of a
competent professional should be sought.

Other Wiley Editorial Offices

John Wiley & Sons Inc., 111 River Street, Hoboken, NJ 07030, USA

Jossey-Bass, 989 Market Street, San Francisco, CA 94103-1741, USA

Wiley-VCH Verlag GmbH, Boschstr. 12, D-69469 Weinheim, Germany

John Wiley & Sons Australia Ltd, 33 Park Road, Milton, Queensland 4064, Australia

John Wiley & Sons (Asia) Pte Ltd, 2 Clementi Loop #02-01, Jin Xing Distripark, Singapore 129809

John Wiley & Sons Canada Ltd, 22 Worcester Road, Etobicoke, Ontario, Canada M9W 1L1

British Library Cataloguing in Publication Data

A catalogue record for this book is available from the British Library

ISBN 0-470-84710-7

Typeset in 12.5/15 pt Garamond by Footnote Graphics, Warminster, Wiltshire.
Printed and bound in Great Britain by Biddles Ltd, Guildford and King's Lynn.
This book is printed on acid-free paper responsibly manufactured from sustainable forestry
in which at least two trees are planted for each one used for paper production.

DEDICATION

To the ladies in my life:
Anne-Marie, Jessica, Chloé and Elodie

Contents

Preface

The more I have worked in marketing, as both a client and a consultant, the more I have come to believe in the old adage: 'It ain't what you do, it's the way that you do it.' In the world of brands and business, as in any competitive arena, every player on the field understands the rules of the game. But although a good grasp of branding theory is important, it is not enough for success. What separates winners from losers is the way people *apply* the theory: attitude counts just as much as ability.

However, most of the multitude of branding books that now exist address the history and theory of brands. They offer much less help on handling the real-life issues of implementation. When I talked to marketing directors, they seemed to agree that there was a need for a more practical workbook on branding and their ideas were the catalyst for *The Brand Gym*. The ultimate sign of success will be if this book ends up sitting on their desks rather than their bedside tables. I hope that highlighter pen, underlining and folded-over corners will be used to mark the most relevant bits.

To get at the real-life issues of boosting brand and business performance, the research for *The Brand Gym* looked not just at successful brands, but also at the people behind this success. As one marketing director aptly put it: 'If you want to learn how to improve your performance in rugby, you don't read a book on the history and theory of the game. You watch the All Blacks in action!' What were the pitfalls that winning teams avoided in growing their brands? What were the *key* factors that explained their superior results? And how did they focus their financial and human resources to get a better return on brand investment? Answers to these questions came from reviewing over 100 consulting projects carried out over the last 10 years. Additional insights came from interviews with 30 leaders of companies such as Apple, Gillette, Egg, Amazon, Starbucks and Bacardi-Martini.

The learning from this research has been distilled into a programme of eight Workouts. These will equip you with simple tools and frameworks to help think through problems, but also suggest the right attitude and mindset with which to apply them. The Workouts have been 'road tested' on coaching programmes with over 100 senior managers and have proven to be effective in the front line of brand building. The principles contained in the

Workouts are powerful for two main reasons. First, they are based on fundamental success factors that are *enduring*, that have stood the test of time and outlived the fads and fashions that have been and gone. Second, they are *universal*, they have worked for teams marketing beer in Russia, tea in America and financial services in the UK.

An overview of *The Brand Gym* programme is shown in Figure 1. It starts by introducing the concept of *Brand-led business*: mobilizing and energizing the whole organization to deliver against a relevant and differentiated brand promise. This is contrasted with the limited role that branding plays for losing teams, who see it as the process of wrapping an image around an often underperforming product or service.

Part II proposes two Workouts to build the *Brand foundations* for growth. 'Get Real' sets the scene for the whole *Brand Gym* approach. It emphasizes the need for pragmatism and business savvy to ensure that strategy is linked to action and is not just a theoretical exercise in 'brand bureaucracy'. 'Search for true insight' then looks at how truths about consumers, brands and markets can help fuel idea creation and how to avoid the pitfalls of research eating up budgets and stifling innovation.

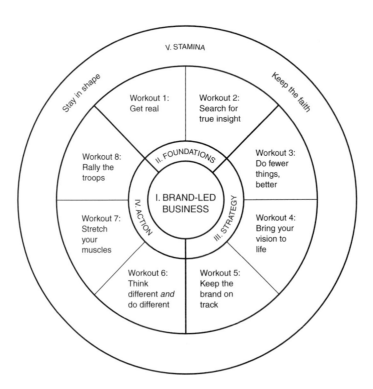

Figure 1: Overview to The Brand Gym programme

Building on these foundations, Part III addresses the core building blocks of *Brand strategy*. 'Do fewer things, better' looks at focusing resources on those brands with the best potential to boost the bottom line. For these core brands, 'Bring your vision to life' then shows how to develop a compelling and inspirational vision. The final strategic building block, 'Keep the brand on track', shows how to guide and inspire the team to develop a coherent, competitive brand mix that helps make this vision a reality.

Part IV of the programme urges teams to translate strategy into the *Brand action* that is ultimately the key to unlocking growth. 'Think different and do different' highlights the need to do things genuinely differently in the marketing mix and not just on paper. 'Stretch your muscles' focuses on the role of brand extension in creating growth. It also flags up the risk of fragmentation, which can dilute returns on marketing investment. 'Rally the troops' then addresses the need to engage and align the whole organization in the brand-building agenda.

The final part of the programme looks at how to create *Brand stamina* to ensure that the momentum of growth is maintained over time. The chapter 'Stay in shape, keep the faith' makes some simple suggestions on how to get the most out of your coaching and training budget.

A summary of the specific, practical problems that the Workouts try to solve is shown in Table 1. A quick scan of these issues will help you get an idea of which Workouts are most relevant to you and so are worth a detailed review. Others may be of less interest and for

Table 1: Overview of issues addressed

Workout	Problem	Solution
1 Get real	Strategy is too theoretical	Ensure that strategy drives action
2 Search for true insight	Expensive consumer research that stifles innovation	Use insight to illuminate and inform, not as a crutch
3 Do fewer things, better	Fragmentation of resources across too many brands	Focus on fewer brands to boost return on investment
4 Bring your vision to life	Vision as a generic statement framed on the wall	Create an ambitious, inspiring vision
5 Keep the brand on track	Brand positioning as theoretical box filling	Positioning to drive a competitive and coherent brand mix
6 Think different *and* do different	Lacking the courage truly to differentiate the brand	Be brave enough to develop a disruptive mix
7 Stretch your brand muscles	Small brand extension 'fiddles' that fragment brand	Launch big, bold extensions to create growth
8 Rally the troops	Reliance on internal communication to create change	Dramatize the vision with real action and align rewards

these you may prefer to read just the 'top and tail': each Workout starts with a one-paragraph summary and ends with three key takeouts and an action plan.

The Brand Gym does not offer a miracle diet capable of transforming you overnight from a fat and flabby couch potato into a world-beating brand athlete. However, with effort and application it will give you a fighting chance of raising your game to a much higher level.

Acknowledgements

Without the marketing directors and general managers with whom I have been lucky enough to work over the last decade, there would be no *Brand Gym*. Their war stories from the front line of brand building are the heart and soul of the book. Several people were key to the birth and early growth of Added Value in Paris: Olivier Charriaud and Huub Van Dorne at Rémy Cointreau; Chris Humphrey, Stephen Knight and Catherine Bacquelin at Walt Disney; Mark Luce at South African Breweries. Others had a direct influence over the development of the Workouts themselves: Andy Bird (now running Brand Learning), David Arkwright and Torvald de Veale at Unilever; Carol Welch at Cadbury; Nick Cross at Egg; Stephen Foulser and Alex Sparks at Blockbuster. Many other managers gave up valuable time to be interviewed for the book and provided many of the case studies: Alan Hely at Apple; Maurice Doyle at Bacardi; Jonathan Sulley at Hasbro; Paul McGarry at Mattel; Paul Curhan at Amazon; Paul Fox at Gillette; Anthony Simon, Fergus Balfour, Simon Clift, Thom Braun and Helen Lewis at Unilever; Phil McManus at Vodafone.

Mark Sherrington of South African Breweries, formerly Chairman of Added Value, had a huge influence over this book. He gave me a big break back in 1993 by hiring me to help set up Added Value's French office, getting me started in the world of consulting. Without him there would have been no clients to work with and so no growth stories to tell. Over the next eight years we spent many an enjoyable and thought-provoking session debating and discussing branding issues and models. He also played a leading role in some of the key projects featured in the book, especially South African Breweries.

Jane Clark, of Jane Clark & Associates put me in touch with Adam Morgan, of Eat the Big Fish fame, without whom *The Brand Gym* would probably still be stuck in my head instead of sitting in your hands. He helped define the concept of a practical, action-driven guide and was good enough to recommend me to his publisher. My subsequent meeting with Rachael Wilkie of John Wiley was one of the highlights of the whole project. Seeing that she shared my enthusiasm for and belief in the project was a huge encouragement. Claire Plimmer later picked up the project and was able to be as enthusiastic and supportive as if she had commissioned the book herself. Sarah Holland of Life Support did just that, by tirelessly and energetically sorting out the many permission and copyright approvals required.

My three guinea pig readers played a critical role in structuring and designing the book. Jonathan Davies of CNN, Tom Allchurch of Fresh Italy and David Nichols of Added Value gave just the right balance of positive encouragement and critical feedback. They suggested features such as the 5-minute Workouts and headline summaries at the start of each chapter. They also encouraged me to stick to the concept of a practical and real-world guide to brand building and stopped me indulging myself in certain sections that sounded more like the diary of a brand consultant.

Last and definitely not least, I have to take my hat off to my wife Anne-Marie. During the four months I dedicated to writing 'my baby' she was looking after our two other brand new babies, Elodie and Chloé, and their big sister Jessica. Anne-Marie never lost her patience and remained my main supporter throughout the sometimes painful process of creation and crafting.

Part I

BRAND-LED BUSINESS

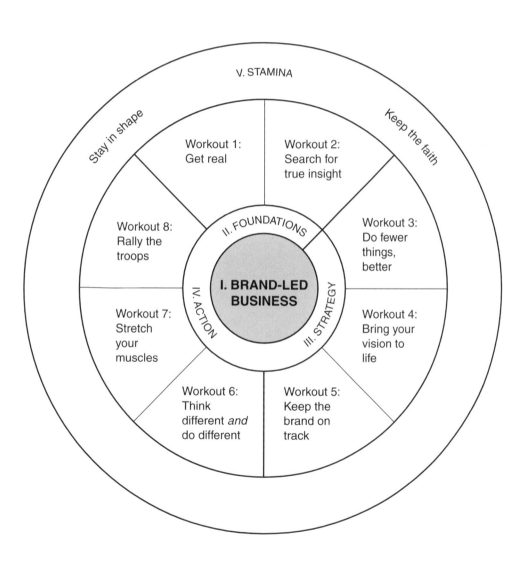

Brand actions speak louder than words

CHAPTER 1

'You can't build a reputation on what you are going to do'.

Henry Ford

 Headlines

Winning teams use 'the brand' as an organizational blueprint for growth that is led from the very top of the company. This 'brand-led business' approach harnesses the full power of branding as a catalyst for growth. In contrast, losing teams see branding in a much more limited role. They mistakenly believe that advertising and design alone can create a 'brand image wrapper' to revive the flagging fortunes of an underperforming product or service.

The brand as image wrapper

Brands are certainly a hot topic for business today: they have starred on the front cover of *The Economist* and even been the subject of an exhibition at the Victoria and Albert Museum in London. An annual report or analyst presentation is now incomplete without the right branding buzzwords. However, many misguided companies expect a new name, fancy logo and flashy advertising campaign by themselves to attract hoards of new customers. The branding process focuses on creating an 'image wrapper', often in the hope of covering up the weaknesses of an underperforming product. This approach to brands that focuses on the exterior look and feel rather than the totality of the product or service can be described as 'outside-in' (Figure 1.1).

A perfect illustration of outside-in thinking is the spate of 're-branding' exercises that many companies have undertaken. Most of these have received justifiable criticism as cosmetic makeovers that cost consumers and shareholders a fortune, without any accompanying change in product performance. One recent example is the re-launch of National

Savings as 'ns&i' for National Savings *and Investments*, which was welcomed by the following review in the national press:

> Its new image features a lower-case logo, ns&i, with a conker in place of the dot above the final letter. MPs of all parties have condemned the makeover, saying it was 'preposterous', 'pointless' and a waste of money. Others called for the institution to improve its saving rates, rather than spend money on a new identity. As an independent financial adviser commented: 'National Savings once represented about 15 per cent of a client's portfolio. But now there are better rates to be had elsewhere. A new logo is not going to entice us' (1).

The shortcomings of outside-in thinking are dramatized by the rapid rise and fall of the dot.com brand pretenders at the end of the 1990s. Not only did they make the fundamental mistake of thinking that a nice name, fancy logo and clever advertising campaign could transform a product into a brand, they went a step further and thought that this could be done overnight if they burnt through enough cash. To help these companies in their outside-in brand-building efforts, there was no shortage of design and advertising agencies. In the majority of cases all they did was help create a 'brand mirage' with no real substance or credibility behind it. The dot.coms soon became dot.bombs and found out the hard way that building brand reputation was much harder than buying brand aware-

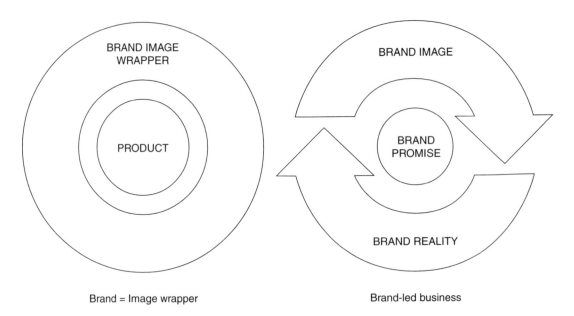

Brand = Image wrapper   Brand-led business

Figure 1.1: Approaches to branding.

ness. The demise of boo.com is perhaps the best example of this folly. A bunch of inexperienced, overpaid executives blew millions of pounds on PR, advertising and graphic design before they even had a website that worked. Getting the right hairstyle for Miss Boo, the virtual sales assistant, seemed a bigger priority for the marketing team than figuring out how to meet the needs of online shoppers. By the time they had ironed out the numerous technical flaws and started selling stuff it was too late, as they had burnt through all the cash and the company went belly up (2).

Bigger, better established companies have also learnt to their cost the problems of an outside-in approach to branding. One such example is the ill-fated global initiative of General Motors to introduce 'brand management' across all its key vehicle lines. With the help of management consultants, a sophisticated process was designed to develop brand positioning strategies for each brand. This started with rigorous market segmentation and then moved on to core consumer targeting and proposition development. The process was then implemented using several rounds of expensive multi-country research for car lines such as the Corsa, Vectra and Frontera. The problem was that the positioning statements that fell out of this process had little or no influence whatsoever on the product development process. Unfortunately, no amount of fancy advertising could make up for poorly performing products. For example, GM in Europe was dogged by problems such as reliability, drive quality and design aesthetics. After several years and many millions of pounds of consultancy fees and research, not to mention thousands of man-hours, the brand management programme was abandoned. Market share in the USA during the four years after the 1996 introduction of brand management actually fell from 32 to 28 per cent (3).

True brands

Four key characteristics help distinguish a true brand and these are summarized in Figure 1.2. First, a true brand does have a distinctive *name and symbol* that are *known* by a large proportion of the target audience. However, these brand identifiers are not only recognized, they are associated with a *trusted customer experience*. Boo.com managed to build lots of buzz and name awareness, but this was not linked to a reputation for customer service. In contrast, Amazon focused from the start on making the process of buying online as easy, quick and enjoyable as possible. This created repurchase levels of over 70 per cent and excellent word of mouth, the most powerful form of brand promotion. Only when the site was working well and its reputation had started to get established did the company turn to

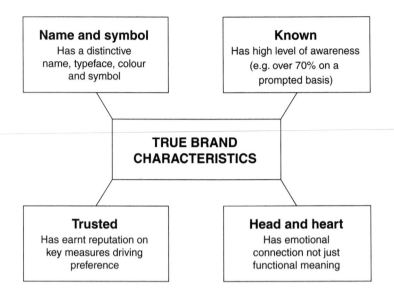

Figure 1.2: Characteristics of a true brand.

expensive above-the-line communication (4). In addition, strong brands have not only functional credentials but also emotional connection: they appeal to the *head and heart*. This is a simple way of separating true brands from products dressed up in brand clothes. The emotional appeal of brands is most obvious when you think of aspirational, lifestyle brands such as Nike, Rolex or Gucci. However, even more everyday favourites such as Oxo, Andrex and Hovis have a human side to them that creates a real bond of affection with consumers.

The business benefits of building true brands are compelling. Research done by Infratest Burke for the Superbrands organization showed just how effective strong brands are at creating loyalty and supporting a price premium. Taking Häagen Dazs as an example, 46 per cent of users said that they intended always to buy this brand and were unlikely to switch. Even more impressive was the fact that 41 per cent said that if the brand was not available they would go elsewhere to find it. Finally, 41 per cent also said that they would not switch to own label no matter how cheap this alternative became (5).

 5-minute workout

Pick at random one or two of the brands in your portfolio and review them against the criteria of a true brand. Do they have a reputation for performance earnt the hard way, by consistently delivering what they promise? Do these brands genuinely appeal to the head and the heart or do they only have a rational, functional side to them, lacking emotional values? Are they brands in a true sense or merely products in disguise?

Brand and deliver

The full potential of branding to drive growth is only realized when it is used to engage and align the resources of the company in delivering value for consumers and shareholders alike. This approach, called 'brand-led business', is defined as follows:

> Leading the organization to consistently deliver against the promise of a motivating and differentiated customer experience.

The brand is no longer an ephemeral image wrapper to be created; it is an organizational blueprint for value creation. The customer experience to be promised and delivered needs careful definition. The real challenge is then to deliver consistently against this promise, an area where many brands tend to fall down, according to research done for *The Brand Gym* by Taylor Nelson in April 2002 among a sample of 1000 UK adults. This showed 60 per cent agreeing that brands tend to promise more than they deliver (Figure 1.3). The study

'Brands tend to promise more than they deliver'

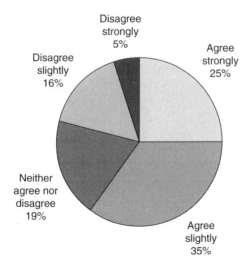

Figure 1.3: *Brand Gym* research on delivery of brand promises.

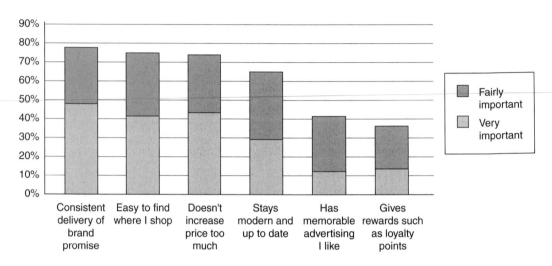

Figure 1.4: *Brand Gym* research on brand loyalty drivers.

also showed the risks for brands that break their promises, with 85 per cent likely to try another brand when this happened. Three-quarters of people would tell a friend, colleague or relative about their bad experience, creating negative word of mouth to harm brand reputation further. On the other hand, the benefits of delivering against your promises were also clear. This was the most important driver of brand loyalty in the survey, with 78 per cent ranking it as important, twice as high as reward schemes (Figure 1.4).

To truly lead the business, brand strategy needs to influence all day-to-day activities, whether they are a high-profile advertising campaign or how helpline supervisors answer the phone. For example, the One-to-One mobile network had a brand strategy all about personal, close relationships captured in an advertising idea of one-on-one conversations. However, its call centre staff used to greet customers by asking them for their mobile number to bring up their details, which was not very close and personal. Contrast this with the way that easyJet staff at the check-in hand back your passport and say 'There you go David', a little gesture that says a lot about the friendly, informal personality of the airline.

Top-level management support is obviously essential if a brand-led business approach is to have any chance of success. Managers need to view key business decisions against financial criteria, but also against the brand promise. This was well summed up by George W. Merck, who said of the company named after him: 'We try never to forget that medicine is for the people. It is not for the profits. The profits follow, and if we have remembered that, they have never failed to appear.' The role of senior management is well illustrated by our first growth story of Tesco, where Terry Leahy played a key role, first as Marketing Director and then as CEO.

The Tesco story

The growth of Tesco during the 1990s allowing it to take leadership of the grocery sector from Sainsbury's is a great example of brand-led business. Advertising from Lowe certainly played a key role and its contribution has been recognized with awards for effectiveness. However, communication was used not to create an image wrapper but to dramatize in a compelling and entertaining fashion a series of truths about the retailer. Success was underpinned by the reinvention of the product itself.

The Tesco turnaround started in the early 1990s with a move away from a historical reputation for 'pile it high, sell it cheap' to a focus on product quality. At this point Tesco had a market share of about 9 per cent, lagging behind Sainsbury's with over 10 per cent. To start putting more emphasis on product selection and quality, an amusing TV campaign featuring Dudley Moore was used. He was shown in an accident-prone search for exclusive products such as free-range hens in France and wine in Italy. Even at this early stage advertising was being employed to make a product promise that consumers could then take up, by going in to buy the eggs or wine that were featured.

A more fundamental change started in 1993 with the rallying call of 'Every little helps'. This phrase has been working hard as an advertising end line for almost a decade. However, its real strength is the way it also works with its staff, showing that each of their actions helps the customer and so helps to build the brand. A total of 114 new initiatives were introduced to help customers. These included mother and baby changing areas, 'One in Front' to open new checkouts at busy times, the Clubcard and a value range (6). Advertising was again used to bring these brand truths to life. Initially communication was fairly straightforward and informative. Emotional appeal was injected from 1995 onwards with the 'Dotty' campaign featuring Prunella Scales. This used the Dotty character and her

Table 1.1: Tesco's growth in UK market share

Market share	1990	1995	1999
Tesco	9.1	13.4	15.4
Sainsbury	10.4	12.2	12.1
Index	88	109	127

long-suffering daughter to demonstrate concrete features that you can try out for yourself, such as the ability to return products, the Clubcard and personal finance offers.

The brand-led business approach has certainly paid off for Tesco (Table 1.1). Over the 1990s it built penetration, loyalty and brand image ratings, resulting in a market share growth of over 50 per cent to take leadership from Sainsbury's (7).

 ## Key takeouts

1 The outside-in view limits the role of branding to that of an image wrapper. This can lead to a disconnect between brand image and brand reality that results in customer disappointment and business decline.
2 Brand awareness can be bought but brand reputation has to be earnt.
3 Brand-led business requires the whole organization to be led from the top to deliver consistently against the brand promise.

 ## 3-part action plan

Today

Ask yourself if the approach to branding in your company means that it is seen as the creation of an image wrapper or used as the organizational blueprint for growth. How do the most senior people in the business think about the concept of 'the brand': are they setting the right example in running a brand-led business? Are there any examples where you are in danger of doing a boo.com and hoping that flashy advertising and imagery can make up for an underperforming product?

This month

Review the different aspects of your business and see how well aligned they are with the brand promise. Do they all work together to help bring the brand promise to life for consumers and earn a reputation for performance? Or are some of them generating sales but not living up to the promise, creating a mismatch between image and reality?

This year

Commit to using Tesco as an example to inspire the development of real substance to underpin your brand. What concrete features or attributes could you add to make a contribution as strong as the 'One in Front' commitment to minimize queuing? Which of these brand substantiators would be worthy of starring in brand communication?

 ## Handover

We now have a clear idea of what 'brand' really means and just how big a challenge running a brand-led business is. We will now move on to look at the brand foundations that are necessary for creating growth. The first Workout, 'Get real', will look at the need to ensure that brand strategy is always linked to action rather than being a theoretical and academic exercise. We will then look at how to 'Search for true insight' about consumers, brands and markets to fuel the strategy creation process.

Part II

BRAND FOUNDATIONS

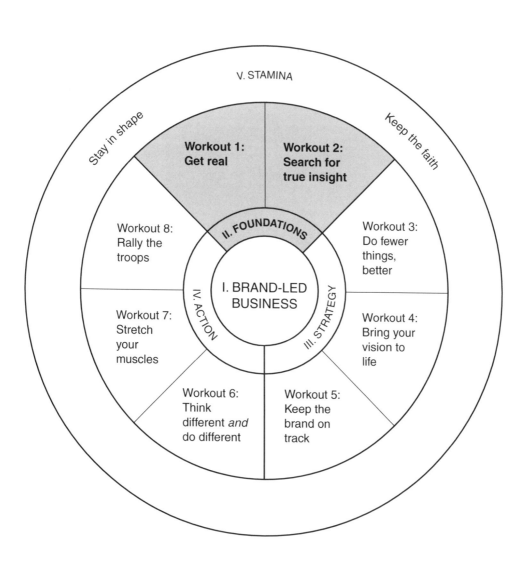

Workout One: Get real

CHAPTER 2

'Great ideas need landing gear as well as wings.'

C.D. Jackson

 ## Headlines

Too many of the discussions about branding are over-intellectual and theoretical, better described as 'brand bureaucracy' than brand building. This strategic posturing is a fruitless exercise that is divorced from the reality of business. Teams need to ensure that brand strategy is always linked to business action. This requires a ruthless focus on those initiatives with the best potential to boost 'return on brand investment'.

Too much of the strategic work on brands is a waste of time and money. As Alan Mitchell says in an article called "The emperor's new clothes": 'No matter how enthusiastic a company's professional marketers may be, amongst engineers, accountants and production line workers, the B-word is still associated with smoke and mirrors and flim-flam.' We will look at three key traps to avoid in brand strategy work: navel gazing, working in a vacuum and pyramid polishing (Figure 2.1)

Navel gazing

The harsh reality is that little of what your brand does will ever make it onto the radar screen of your target consumers. Therefore, you need constantly and ruthlessly to prioritize the activities of your team to ensure that it concentrate on things that will make a difference to the bottom line. This is necessary because your team members are so close to their brand that they may overestimate the importance of the issues on which they are working. They fail to appreciate how small a role many brands really play in the lives of the people who buy and use them. Many of the decisions they are agonizing over have no direct impact on the amount of coffee or cornflakes that the factory ships.

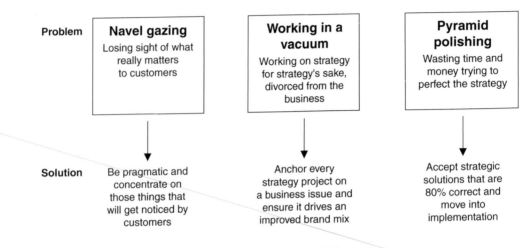

Figure 2.1: The risks of brand bureaucracy and how to avoid them.

The need to focus on the things that will boost return on brand investment is bigger than ever in today's business world. Most teams have more on their plate than they can handle, with the level of brand complexity getting bigger and the intensity of competition getting hotter. What is more, the plate itself is shrinking, with the threat of recession putting downward pressure on both headcount and marketing budgets.

One example of navel gazing occurred when United Biscuits (UB) France bought the Delacre biscuit business. It inherited a range of tin boxes called Tea Time that contained a selection of different Delacre biscuits. The UB team spent a considerable amount of time debating what to do with the Tea Time brand and how much importance to give to it on packaging versus the Delacre name. Different mock-ups were developed and compared. Media strategies were discussed. Tea Time advertising was created. However, a consumer in a focus group brought the team back down to earth when she was asked what type of biscuits she bought and replied: '*Les boittes Delacre*' (Delacre tins). A quick awareness study confirmed that the Tea Time name was actually known by only a minority of consumers. It was not a brand in a true sense but rather a range descriptor that was used by some but not all buyers. The Delacre name was made more prominent on packaging and benefited from renewed support, with Tea Time relegated to its rightful role as a product descriptor.

Range naming is one of the most common forms of navel gazing. Teams spend time and money creating fancy names and even logos when most of us actually refer to 'the blue one, not the red one' when navigating through a product range. However, the problem can also be seen in many other areas of brand building.

5-minute workout

Imagine that an aggressive and bottom-line-focused hostile bidder is taking over your company. If it wanted to strip out costs in order to boost the bottom line, where would it look first? Challenge yourself to ask some hard questions about where you are spending your money and where you are adding value, and check that these are one and the same.

Working in a vacuum

This trap occurs when managers start to see strategy as an exercise that has value in its own right, rather than as a means to the end of profitable growth. This leads to the 'brand think' of strategic work becoming artificially separated from the 'brand do' of implementation. Many international companies have created international brand management teams that are supposed to coordinate local teams in an attempt to create a consistent brand. In reality, many of the central teams become 'brand bureaucrats' who work on strategy that is not linked to the business-building efforts of operating companies.

Another example of brand bureaucracy is how one major food company required the completion of a 'brand onion' strategy tool for every one of its brands. This huge exercise ate up the brand and advertising agency teams' valuable time. However, in many cases there was no advertising, or any other marketing, planned for the brand in question. In other words, the brand positioning over which the team had slaved was a purely theoretical box-filling exercise with no marketing or business purpose whatsoever. It was nice to have all the boxes completed in line with strict company guidelines, but the thing was of no practical use to anyone. Brand think was completely divorced from brand do.

On any brand strategy project it is important to start with the end in mind by clarifying how the work will affect the brand mix. Framing the project as a business issue, such as 'brand revitalization' or 'growth acceleration', helps remind people that the strategy is merely a first step on the journey to growth, not the end point. Knowing which bits of the brand mix will be driven by the new strategy also enables you to involve the right agency people from the start. Most projects will eventually require new communication, in which case getting the ad agency on board from day one is crucial. Failing to do so runs the risk that they will lack the understanding and commitment needed to implement effectively. Secondly, any stimulus material used to explore alternative strategies can incorporate examples of the sort of creative work that will be in the final mix. A proposition might look great on paper, but will it work in press advertising or on a piece of packaging? Finally, as the creative agencies are involved from the start, they can experiment with rough ideas for execution as the strategy evolves.

On a project for South African Breweries developing a new brand of beer for Russia, the agency developed and tested rough storyboards towards the end of the brand strategy work and was able to identify a lead route. The learning from this work even allowed fine-tuning of the strategy, which made it even stronger. Different packaging ideas for each strategic direction had also been developed and explored and the final design selected. So at the end of the strategy project the team had a finalized brand positioning but also a pack design and rough storyboard. This use of 'parallel processing' meant that the work was done in the space of only five months, including quantitative validation, the time many strategic projects would take without getting near to any mix development.

Polishing the pyramid

Belief in the fairytale world of marketing encourages teams to perfect the strategy and test it to death before using it to brief on mix development such as advertising or packaging. The search for the perfect strategy wastes valuable time and energy and can delay the project to such an extent that nimbler competition gets to market first. In this mythical process marketing follows a tidy, neat and logical path (Figure 2.2). This starts with understanding consumers followed by strategy development and testing. A perfected and validated strategy is used to brief research and development, who come up with a great product, which you then advertise exhaustively.

However, the reality is much more messy and unstructured. Many strategies for great brands are modified to reflect learning in the market. Some teams spend months trying to craft and perfect a brand essence that distils the brand idea down to a few words. Nevertheless, it is often in the creative expression of the brand in advertising that those elusive, powerful and resonant words emerge. The European Marketing Director of Amazon told how the time pressure of the dot.com world forced him to dash off the positioning in a day, whereas the same result would have taken several months in his previous company.

A better approach is to 'launch and learn' by accepting a strategy that is 80 per cent correct and then trying it out in the market to learn about its true effectiveness. In the process mistakes may be made, but teams will learn more from this than from any number of consumer tests. 'Bottling the magic' then involves capturing learning on what is

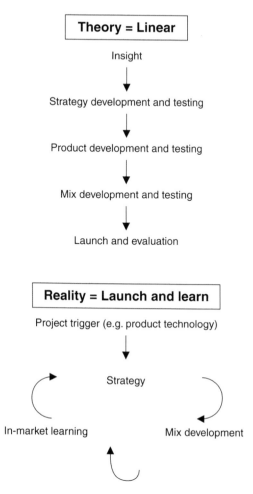

Figure 2.2: Theory and reality of brand building.

working in the marketplace and using this to update the strategy. Often it is little things in the mix itself that turn out to be the keys to growth. Take the Andrex brand of toilet tissue that has dominated the UK market for several decades. A huge part of the brand's enduring appeal is the way a cute little puppy has helped imbue something as mundane as a toilet roll with a personality. The puppy first appeared during a 1970s advert playing a supporting role, simply as one part of a family setting. However, the marketing team discovered that it generated a massive amount of consumer interest and recall. They were smart enough to pick up on this happy accident and make the puppy a more central part of the brand's communication. Thirty years later the puppy is still going strong, taking pride of place on the pack, coming to life in the form of promotional toys and continuing to feature in advertising. You can bet that it is now one of the most important elements of the positioning. You can be just as sure that it was nowhere to be seen in the original strategy.

Bringing out the real issues

A brand-led business briefing template can help bring to the surface the real business and implementational issues on a brand strategy project and ensure that the team stays true to the principles of the 'Get real' Workout. An example is shown in Table 2.1 from a real-life project on the Cointreau brand of orange spirit done by Added Value. This helped clarify that although the project was initially described as a brand equity assessment, this was just the first step towards defining a new positioning as a contemporary drink for younger consumers. In turn, the re-positioning strategy was needed to help brief on new advertising and packaging. Having a clear end in mind ensured that the right team and process were put in place, not only to understand where the brand was but also to develop ideas of where it could go. An advertising and design agency was quickly brought on board to help in creating the re-launch mix. Finally, a clear idea of the measures of success meant that tracking could be planned to see if the re-launch was working.

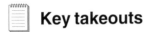 **Key takeouts**

1 Too much strategy work is closer to brand bureaucracy than brand building. Care should be taken to ensure that brand think is always closely linked to brand do.
2 Navel gazing can lead teams to overestimate the importance of issues on which they are working.
3 The search for the perfect strategy can lead to pyramid polishing when a better approach would be to launch and learn.

 **3-part action plan**

Tomorrow

Do a quick review of the brand strategy projects that your team is currently working on, such as brand portfolio strategy, visioning or positioning. For each of these projects, use the business briefing tool to critique them and check that they are anchored in the pragmatic reality of business and are not just theoretical exercises. If a project is not clearly linked to the marketing mix and will not drive the business forward in a very concrete way, then re-work it, shelve it or kill it. You will be liberating valuable time and money to concentrate on other projects.

Table 2.1: Brand-led business briefing template

Business issue	What is the business problem or opportunity that has prompted this project: *Sales of Cointreau have been in decline for the last 15 years, with volume sales in 1995 halved versus their peak in 1980. This reflects the ageing of the user base, with half of consumers over 45, and the failure to bring in new, younger users.*
Brand issue	What is the brand issue you are trying to solve and how will the solution help address the business issue? *The brand has excellent awareness and distribution and is appreciated for being an authentic brand with real heritage. However, it has become dusty and out of date, locked in people's minds into the after-dinner sipping moment.*
Consumer evidence	What qualitative and quantitative learning helps support the brand issue? *Qualitative learning shows the brand personality to be old-fashioned and lacking dynamism. Quantitative data shows the old skew in the user base and the mismatch between the brand's image and key needs on items such as 'easy to drink', 'mixability' and 'youthfulness'.*
Strategy application	What will the strategy be used for? Specifically, which bits of the marketing mix will it guide and inform and when will these hit the market? *The strategy will be used to brief for a complete re-launch of the brand mix, in particular packaging, advertising and point of sale.*
Internal stakeholders	Who are the key influencers and users of the strategy? How will you get them on board? *Five key European markets account for 75% of global volumes and it is essential that the general managers and marketing directors of these markets are brought on board. The US is a small but growing business and so is also important.*
Agency teams	Which are the key agencies who will be expected to use the strategy and how will you get them actively involved? *The key agencies are Dragon Rouge for packaging and BBH for advertising. They will both be part of the team to whom the positioning exploration results will be presented and they will use these to develop the briefs for the new brand mix.*
Measurement	How will the effectiveness of the project be judged both in brand and business terms? *Business terms: return to volume growth of at least 2–4% per year. Brand terms: 5% improvement in brand image scores, 10% increase in ever used scores, increase in share of volume consumed by under 35s from 35% to 50%.*
Prototyping	How do you plan to bring the strategy to life so that you can explore it with consumers and the business team? *Positioning ideas will be illustrated using mood boards and if possible mock-ups of new packaging graphics to bring the new brand personality to life.*

Also, ask how long the team has been working on the project. If the answer is more than three months, then challenge team members to prove that they are still adding value. If the explanation turns out be pyramid polishing and box filling, then help the team nail the strategy to at least 80 per cent completion and move on to mix development. Another common reason for projects dragging on is the tendency to research them to death. Could the answers come from existing data and research? Or could a judgement call be made now to allow the project to carry on to execution with a 'disaster check' being done in parallel? By taking a more pragmatic approach you will speed up the process and make it leaner and less heavy to manage.

This month

Ensure that the day-to-day work of the team stays focused on things that will have an impact on the bottom line and is not spent navel gazing. Before allocating valuable time in a meeting to discuss a brand issue, check whether your consumers are likely to care about the issue or whether it will disappear in the blur of the weekly shopping trip. Also, think about what meetings, projects or processes could be chopped without any difference to the business. You may be surprised to find that many bits of the process take place simply because they always have!

This year

Over a year you have more chance to make some significant changes to the way you run your brand or business. Start to think about the need for business savvy and pragmatism when hiring new people for your team. Is the candidate able to see how branding can help build the business, or are they a brand bureaucrat, more divorced from reality? Ensure that the principles of 'Get real' are part of the performance review for your team, as they are often left out in favour of other more common criteria such as creativity, leadership and team working skills. Finally, make sure that your team is actively linked in to the rest of the business team and not falling into the ivory tower syndrome. Don't wait for a project workshop or the annual planning process to get other functions involved, seek them out proactively and try to see problems through their eyes.

Handover

The principles of 'Get real' are the bedrock of brand-led business. Applying them to all areas of marketing will help ensure that activities are growing the business and not falling into the trap of brand bureaucracy. One of the key areas where this can happen is consumer research, which can end up slowing down projects and eating up too much money. The next Workout will look at how to avoid these pitfalls and ensure that the focus is on a 'Search for true insight'.

Workout Two: Search for True Insight

CHAPTER 3

'Moins de tests et plus de testicules! (Less tests, more testosterone.)'

French creative director

 ## Headlines

True insight into consumers, brands and markets is a springboard for idea generation and a stimulus for growth. However, over-reliance on consumer research can have the opposite effect, stifling innovation and wasting both time and money. Teams should not rely solely on research to explore and evaluate ideas but rather look for cheaper and better ways of searching for insight. In particular, they should look to build empathy with the target consumer and experience through experimenting and prototyping.

The drunk and the lamppost

Insight can be a great source of ideas and innovation. Staying in touch with what is happening in your consumers' world is vital if you are to create products and services that meet their needs and wants. Understanding markets and how they are evolving is crucial to ensure that your product offer is adapted and improved to stay ahead of the competition. Ask the guys at *Encyclopaedia Britannica* about what happens when you fail to do this. Mention Encarta or CD-Rom and watch them weep. However, contrary to what many people believe, consumer research is only one way to generate insights and in some cases is not even the best one.

Managers in many big companies use research in the same way a drunk uses a lamppost: for support not illumination. 'Let's do a few groups', 'Why don't we talk to a few more consumers?' or 'I don't know, put it in a test' are all common responses to difficult brand issues where research is used as a crutch. This bogs down projects, slowing them up and eating through huge amounts of money. In today's accelerated world it means that there is also a risk that faster, more self-confident competitors will be launching while you are waiting for the latest research report. Some of the most important limitations and risks are inno-kill, hot housing, scratching the surface and being a rear-view mirror.

Innokill

The most dangerous aspect of research is the way it can kill innovation and new ideas. The worst example of this is perhaps the quantitative tests used to 'screen' innovation ideas at a very early stage. Often new ideas are illustrated with a primitive line drawing, or even no picture at all, and shown to a bunch of average consumers for evaluation. This does not do justice to the ideas and, as with most innovation, the man or woman in the street is unlikely to go for them at first viewing. The result in many cases is a low 'top box' score, the percentage of people saying they would *definitely* buy the product. However, launch conditions for the new idea would be different with attractive packaging, heavy advertising and adoption by more adventurous consumers all giving it a better chance of success. If the team are not passionate about the idea and ready to defend it despite the disappointing results, the concept can die a premature death.

If you do have to research an idea at an early stage, take some of the budget and invest it in developing a proper prototype. This will bring the idea to life for you, the consumer and also the rest of the business team. It will have a better chance of getting support from the internal team and be more likely to survive its first innokill test. The Post-it™ note bombed in its early tests and in a less innovative company than 3M it may never have made it to market. Not surprisingly it got nuked in research when presented as a written concept: 'New! A rectangular piece of paper you can write on and stick everywhere.' However, when the notes were prototyped and given out to people in the 3M offices, they created a huge buzz and people were clambering to get hold of them. A wider sampling test in surrounding offices confirmed the product's potential.

Beyond prototyping, other survival tips include recruiting at least one part of the test sample among consumers who are more receptive to new products. Also, adding some qualitative exit interviews with people who loved the concept and those who hated it will give you valuable nuances as to why the concept was working or not.

Hot housing

Research has a tendency to blow things out of proportion by making people focus on stuff that would normally sail right over their head. Research is used to explore differences in concepts, packaging or advertising that are so small as to be invisible under real conditions. After staring at two slightly different packs for fifteen minutes in a focus group with a bright light being shined in your face, *you* might come up with a point of view about which you prefer. However, on the race round the supermarket with the kids in tow, would you spot the difference?

This problem was experienced when Heinz tested new packaging for its range of soups with consumers. After seeing first the current and then the new version, brand users were up in arms at the proposed changes. The problem was of course magnified by seeing the 'before' and 'after' packs side by side, something that would not happen on the shelf. The design agency was convinced that the changes were needed to update the brand graphics and had a clever trick up their sleeve to prove it. In the next round of focus groups they showed the *new* pack first and it got favourable feedback, seen as being familiar yet a little more modern and fresh. They then showed the *current* pack, which was rejected outright as being old-fashioned. So, if you are going to magnify something, at least make sure that it's the opportunity rather than the problem.

The other problem caused by hot housing is the failure to take into account the learning effect that goes on when a product or campaign is launched. People are asked to react to a single exposure of an idea and then discuss it for two to three hours. In the real world, they would have multiple exposures, each lasting only 30 seconds. The team working on Heineken in the 1970s understood this shortcoming of research when it reviewed the disastrous results on a new advertising campaign. The idea of 'Heineken refreshes the parts other beers cannot reach' was met with huge resistance on first showing, as it broke all the rules of beer advertising. Gone were the three mates down the pub ordering their favourite brew from a busty barmaid. Instead, there was a line of policemen wiggling their tired toes back to life, helped by a refreshing drink of Heineken. The team was brave enough to ignore the results, based on a belief that the British public would grow to first learn and then to love the idea. That intuition proved to be right and the campaign went on to be one of the most successful ever, building both sales and brand image over many years.

Scratching the surface

Do *you* really know how you brush your teeth every day and why you buy the brand of toothpaste you do? What about your shampoo or deodorant? The answer for most of us is that we haven't the foggiest idea, yet brand teams rely on research to get consumers to tell them answers to these sorts of questions every day. The problem with focus groups and other similar techniques is that they work at a rational level, asking people to remember what they do and try to explain why. Putting eight people together rather than talking to them one on one of course makes this problem worse. They not only struggle to remember stuff locked away in their memory, they may also start to posture and not tell the truth if this is embarrassing. I saw this for myself when doing focus groups on the glamorous subject of male underwear. All eight guys claimed to wear grey, Calvin Klein-esque boxer shorts. I got them to pull down their trousers at the end of the group and reveal the truth of the recruitment questionnaire they had each filled in. This showed that most of them were wearing big, baggy white pants, with two being secret Hom posing pouch fans!

A better way of getting a true insight is to observe people *in situ* as they use the product, a technique that borrows from the disciplines of anthropology and ethnography. On a project for CNN to gain more understanding of the needs and attitudes of the international business traveller, the use of focus groups was considered. However, the team was worried about the lack of colour and depth that this would have provided. Instead, people were filmed in real situations, in their hotel room, at the airport or in the office. This was more effective at bringing to life issues such as the need for a short, sharp summary of key headlines, and the desire to be 'in the know' for the next day's meeting.

Research is a rear-view mirror

Despite the advances made in research, it still looks backwards on the world. In the same way that you cannot drive a car by looking in a rear-view mirror, you need more forward visibility to run a business. However sophisticated the technique, qualitative or quantitative, it is based on people's perception of the world today and cannot take into account what will happen tomorrow. Consider the shampoo brand Pantene, which has become one of the UK's favourites. Back in 1988 it was being tested before launch and *people hated it*. 'The name sounds like underpants!' they protested in focus groups, vowing never to buy it. These views were backed up by hard data, with the advertising pre-tests showing some of the worst results on record. So what did Procter and Gamble (P&G) do? Give up on the launch? Change the name? No, the launch went ahead as planned, a key part of making Pantene one of P&G's key global hair brands. It was possible to filter out some of the negative effects of the name on the test results to get a clearer read. An advertising campaign with acceptable results was finally developed. However, the biggest factor in going ahead was a belief that with a heavily supported launch and great product, the brand would break through the consumer barriers to trial.

Think about some of the other innovations that might have seemed strange at the time. Brakes that switch on and off (ABS), a fashionable plastic watch that costs £30 (Swatch) and a bank without branches (First Direct) have now all become integral parts of everyday life. These successes show that sometimes you need to back your beliefs, not the findings of conventional research, especially when ideas break new ground.

 ## 5-minute workout

Imagine that the research budget for your brand was cut to zero. What ways would you use to generate nuggets of insight about consumers, brands and markets? How would you go about getting some measure of the potential of new products or services to give you the confidence to invest behind them? If you then got back one-third of the budget, which bits of research would you add back? For the other two-thirds, ask some tough questions about how essential they really are and if there aren't cheaper and better ways of getting the same answers.

Fear of failure

The longer-term effects of the addiction to research are even more serious for an organization. It raises the risk of managers becoming brand bureaucrats, briefing and analysing research instead of building a finely tuned sense of intuition and business judgement. This results in a fear of failure, which leads to conservatism and an inability to make decisions without the props of data and testing. Managers never take off with their own wings to explore new ideas and innovations.

To illustrate the problem of fear of failure, consider the simple test in Table 3.1. It shows how a company under different circumstances will rate a manager working on a new product. Try the test for yourself.

First, consider what happens if the manager launches the product. If it fails, how many 'brownie points' out of 10 would he get (i.e. how much reward, recognition and prospects for promotion)? Write it in the top left box. And what about if it succeeds? The number goes in the top right box. Consider the case where he delays and does not launch, but the competitor does. Again, allocate points out of 10 for product failure and success. Now, add

Table 3.1: Ratings for a new product manager

	Product fails	Product succeeds	Total
GO FOR IT AND LAUNCH	Points out of 10	Points out of 10	Out of 20
DELAY AND COMPETITOR LAUNCHES	Points out of 10	Points out of 10	Out of 20

up along the rows the total points for launching and the total for not launching and letting the competition go first.

The results of having done this many times with brand teams from major multinationals are shown in Table 3.2 and make for depressing reading. People get punished for launching and failing more than if they sit on their research while the competitor moves and wins. The net result is a greater incentive for delaying and waiting than acting and doing.

Table 3.2: Typical results

	Product fails	Product suceeds	Total
GO FOR IT AND LAUNCH	2 out of 10	7 out of 10	**9 points**
DELAY AND COMPETITOR LAUNCHES	7 out of 10	5 out of 10	**12 points**

Although an over-reliance on research can be bad for you, true consumer insight can be incredibly powerful, as shown by the development of Golden Barrel, a new beer to help South African Breweries (SAB) enter Russia (Table 3.3). This successful launch shows how non-research-based techniques can provide the most valuable nuggets of insight and also how a team needs to rely on its own judgement to make difficult calls, even when quantitative testing is carried out.

The Golden Barrel story

The Golden Barrel story starts back in early 1998 after SAB had spent many millions of dollars to buy a mothballed brewery just outside Moscow. A monumental effort started to transform it into a modern facility that met SAB's best production standards. At the same time the new European Marketing Director, Mark Luce, began work in earnest to create a new brand from scratch, helped by consultancy Added Value. The brief was literally a sheet of white paper, with no consumer, market or brand learning available and no Russian team yet in place to help provide any insights. Furthermore, the entire brand creation process had to be completed by the end of the year to allow time for production ahead of the peak beer season the following spring. This meant that there was eight months to do everything from initial research through to strategy development and into brand mix creation, including naming, packaging and advertising.

One of the biggest challenges was building an intimate knowledge of the Russian consumer and the role that beer could play in what was traditionally a vodka market. Scratching the surface was not enough, the team needed to dig much deeper to understand how to connect with consumers at both a rational and emotional level. *Cultural analysis* helped

Table 3.3: Insight techniques and findings on Golden Barrel

Technique	Example of findings	Action
1 Review of literature on the Russian people and their culture	Importance of '*posidel ki*', being in touch with people; there is no word in Russian for 'privacy'	Show beer as a shared experience and not solitary
2 Decoding of popular entertainment that featured beer	Beer is a light, refreshing drink versus the serious, hard drink of vodka	Tone should be light-hearted and carefree
3 Observation of people drinking in the street	Beer is drunk direct from the bottle by young people	Show drinking from bottle not glass in communication
4 Qualitative exploration of packaging prototypes	Quality cues are important to justify price premium	Use of gold foil on neck and label
5 Quantitative 'session tasting' of different beers	Guidance on optimum level of gas and bitterness	Finalization of product specification
6 Qualitative groups with different life stages	Leading brand Baltika seen as artificial and not close to them	Make brand more approachable and in touch with Russian drinkers
7 Accompanied drinking sessions	Beer as a 'five-minute holiday' to escape from the pressures of life	Portray this feeling of escape and freedom in advertising
8 Street visits to see small market stalls where beer is sold	Limited shelf space and facings	Importance of variants to get shelf space, need for high impact of pack
9 Quantitative segmentation study	Sizing of key segments, validation of key needs	Confirmed focus on growing segment of younger male drinkers
10 Price elasticity	Confirmed volume target could be delivered at a 10% price premium	Gave confidence to launch at price premium

understand fundamental aspects of the Russian people, such as the importance of being in touch with other people and not being alone. This had a direct impact on the TV advertising, which portrayed three guys sharing a beer (three is said to be the best number as a drunk can be supported by one friend on either side!).

Decoding of how beer was portrayed in popular entertainment showed that the drink was a light and refreshing beverage compared to the hard-edged, serious side of vodka. Therefore, the tone of the brand's communication needed to be light-hearted and to emphasize the refreshing aspect of the product. This finding was confirmed by *observation* of people drinking beer in the street straight from the bottle as if it were a soft drink. This informal way of drinking was incorporated into the launch commercial.

However, perhaps the most valuable nugget of insight came from an *accompanied drinking session* after a focus group in Moscow had finished. One of the group offered to take the researcher for a beer with his friends, and they huddled in the cold on a bench in front of his apartment building. They would normally drink here as most apartments were too small to have friends round and bars were too expensive. As the group chatted, one of them jokingly said how a good beer was a 'five-minute holiday' from the hardship of everyday life in Russia. This inspired a communication concept showing brand users escaping from the city on what seemed to be a beach, but turned out to be a train transporting sand. Golden Barrel inspired them to find a clever way of having a good time together.

The team also used *quantitative research* in the right way to inform but not to decide. Towards the end of the project a quantitative test was used to compare two pack designs and the results of the test showed that they were neck and neck. Some teams would have been stuck and even considered another test or more detailed analysis. However, the Golden Barrel team had a clear point of view before the test on which pack was stronger, based on its experience of the beer market. This meant the team members quickly agreed on the right one to back, confident that it had performed well in the test but also believing instinctively that it was the right way forward.

The launch went ahead on time in the spring of 1999. Golden Barrel set a new benchmark in quality through SAB's brewing expertise. This allowed a more consistent taste delivery and so provided a strong functional underpinning, helping the brand win several consumer magazine awards. The communication connected emotionally with the consumer in a way that advertising had not done before. It showed an intimate understanding of the beer-drinking moment and what it meant to Russian men. The tagline 'We should meet more often' became part of Russian everyday language and was featured in TV programmes. Golden Barrel went on to be the most successful beer launch that SAB had ever done, with 1 million hectolitres of sales being more than twice the forecast.

The Golden Barrel story shows how insight can be used to both inspire and inform brand teams in their search for growth. We will now look in more detail at these two issues and the role that research can play.

Beyond exploration to empathy

Winning teams in *The Brand Gym* research used true, deep insight into consumers as a stimulus for brand development, but understood that research could only get them so far.

True insight requires more than merely understanding consumers, you need to get much closer to the action to feel the insight in your gut, not just understand it in your head. You need to get beyond only doing consumer exploration and build 'consumer empathy' (Figure 3.1). This requires breaking down of the artificial separation that can still exist between the people who use products ('the consumer') and the people who sell them ('the brand'). The mirror separating you from the eight people normally recruited to participate in focus groups illustrates this divide. This encourages brand teams to see the consumer as living on a completely different planet and almost speaking a different language, with the need for a 'moderator' to translate findings into client speak.

In addition, building consumer empathy is not something you do every now and then. It is a way of seeing the world and being open to new opportunities whenever they may spring up. Take the example of the PG Tips 'chimps' advertising campaign that ran for over 30 years in the UK (Figure 3.2). It helped grow and sustain share in the face of intense competition, build brand equity and maintain a price premium. A copywriter working on the brief back in 1956 was in Regent's Park Zoo when he chanced on the chimpanzee's tea party being enjoyed by a huge crowd. He was intrigued by the human-like way in which the chimps drank their cuppa and just how funny people found their exploits. This insight provided the spark for one of the most successful pieces of consumer marketing ever, generating an estimated £125 million of additional revenue over a 20-year period (1).

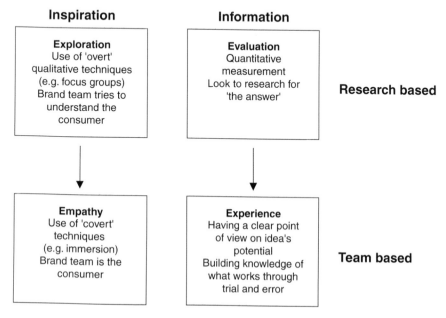

Figure 3.1: Different approaches to insight generation.

Figure 3.2: The PG chimps.

Don't understand the consumer, be the consumer

The visceral, emotional nature of an insight that you feel in the gut is what differentiates it from a run-of-the-mill finding. This deeper-level understanding was illustrated in the Golden Barrel story, where really empathizing with the Moscow beer drinker gave a more three-dimensional picture of his life, hopes and fears. But the best way to get true insight is to be the consumer yourself, or at least to have a real enthusiasm for and interest in the category.

This goes against the grain of the training at P&G. We were taught that you could have an insight about any category if you had access to the right data and the ability to analyse it correctly. My first job as a brand manager was on the Milton brand of sterilizing fluid and tablets for use in cleaning baby feeding bottles. Pouring over the data in the fact book and attending focus groups with new mums and dads helped me with consumer exploration. But no matter how hard I tried, as a single 25-year-old guy enjoying life in London, it was a big if not impossible stretch to feel in my gut what it was like to be a parent; I could not build real consumer empathy. Only as a new dad a decade later did I really feel the responsibility of having a small baby, the fear of not sterilizing the bottles correctly and the sheer joy of seeing a happy, healthy newborn.

Building consumer empathy is not a quick fix and requires changes to the way people are recruited. Those at Amazon, Starbucks and Egg have a genuine interest in the market, are enthused by the mission of the company and tend to be loyal users of the product. I would never get hired at Nike as I am a Saturday sports spectator, not a passionate and active participant. In a consumer goods business where you change brands it may be harder always to have this level of connection with the category and the consumer. However, you can try to influence the assignments you get and also ensure that you spend more time with consumers *in situ*. When training Unilever brand managers we could always spot the guy or girl working on Lynx/Axe, as they were dressed more fashionably and had a better grasp of the language of youth. Research can help you uncover deep insights, but it needs to use unconventional techniques to go 'under cover'.

Going undercover

Most qualitative research techniques are constrained by their use of overt questioning to generate learning, with the limitations we have seen. When you do use research you need to be more covert to get deeper and truer insights. Ways to do this include immersion, cultural decoding, changing the brand's clothes and prototyping.

Immersion

Immersing yourself in the world of the consumer and a brand can be more useful than a bunch of focus groups. On one drinks brand project the advertising proposed by a hot London agency was clever, but went straight over the head of the young working-class target. 'Don't they get it?' exclaimed the hurt creative director, where in fact it was he who didn't get it. Sat in his Soho office he was a million miles away from the 19-year-olds in Amsterdam and Hamburg to whom the advertising needed to talk. The team was changed to a couple of 20-year-olds who spent a brilliant weekend attending foam parties and booze cruises to experience the brand *in situ*. Within a fortnight they had cracked the brief and got a storyboard approved. An even simpler way of getting close to consumers is to talk to real people about the product, not only marketing people. The 'secretary test' is a cheap and effective way of getting real-life, instant feedback and friends and family can also be valuable sources of findings.

Decoding

Decoding communication and broader cultural codes can lead to valuable information. On the Golden Barrel project many of the insights about the potential role that beer could play came from decoding the way the product was portrayed in popular culture. On an Added Value project for Freeserve, the UK's leading Internet service provider, decoding the way in which the Internet was referred to on television showed how people's attitudes to it were evolving. From a time when it was featured only on scientific programmes, the Net had gone mainstream. You knew it had finally become part of everyday life when it was the subject of a conversation in the Britain's favourite soap opera, *Eastenders*. This led the Freeserve team to adapt its communication to focus less on educating people about what the Internet was and more on the specific benefits of the Freeserve brand.

Changing the brand's clothes

When trying to understand the potential of a brand to evolve and innovate, it is hard to get past consumers' current perceptions of the brand. If questioned overtly they will play back imagery based on past experience. When working on the Cointreau brand of orange liqueur, focus groups helped paint a colourful picture of the brand's reality. People personified the brand as 'A French aristocrat who lives in a run-down chateau and drives a rusty Rolls-Royce. No one comes to visit him any more and he is very lonely.' This reflected the lack of innovative brand marketing and a perception that the product was a strong, heavy and sickly after-dinner drink. This showed the heritage and roots of the brand, but didn't get the team much further. Changing the brand's clothes gave a more interesting insight into the appeal of the product itself. The advertising agency, BBH, sampled the product with people and captured their negative reactions on film. They then sampled the same Cointreau product, but this time in an Absolut Orange bottle. Suddenly young people loved the product, finding it sharp, clean and tasty. This covert piece of research dramatized the fact that with a revamped brand personality and image the underlying product had a real chance of winning over new drinkers.

Prototyping

Mocking up ideas is another way of getting ideas under consumers' radar screens. By bringing to life an idea you can get round some of the scepticism that may greet a concept by showing it as if it already existed. You can say, 'Here is what the brand is doing in another part of the country, it already exists.' In the case of a product brand this can be a mocked-up package showing what the idea would look like. For a service brand you can bring to life the change in customer experience that would result from a new positioning, for example. In the case of a new strategy for a hotel, there might one direction around the idea of 'responsiveness' and another around 'personalization'. If these ideas stay in written concept form they would be hard for a prospective customer to understand. A much more effective solution is to mock up examples of hotel services that would be offered in each case. For the responsiveness direction this could be features such as full 24-hour room service or your own butler to wait on your every need and want.

One project where prototyping was an essential ingredient was the creation of the Egg brand, back in 1998. This was a project where overtly asking 'Would you place your savings with an Internet bank called Egg?' would have been a sure-fire way of committing innokill.

The Egg story

You have to try quite hard to think back to the way the world of financial services was in 1998, when there was no Goldfish, Cahoot, IF and the like. Banking was a boring business and the Internet was still in its infancy for most people.

The Prudential had decided that there was a real opportunity for a new type of financial services proposition that treated consumers more as equals and less as servants. It would also be delivered in a fresher and more exciting way. The brand would have no branches and would do business over the telephone and Internet, to cut out costs and also give a more contemporary feel. As with most innovations the brand name was a major issue: do you use a known and trusted name like Prudential or go for a new name? There were strong arguments for a name such as pru.com, which would have allowed the group to tap into the equity of the Prudential brand but give it a new twist for the Internet age. However, this route didn't feel a big enough step, and the stretch between the image of the Prudential and the new brand was too big. So a new name was the route ahead and efforts to generate one began in earnest.

Egg was one of a shortlist of names that was on the table when design agency Brown KSDP was briefed on the project. The team felt that the Egg name had great possibilities, as it was simple, easy to remember and broke all the codes of the stuffy banking world. But would people really invest their hard-earned savings in a bank called Egg? The team mocked up the brand as it might look after launch, with Egg credit cards, chequebooks and advertising. The prototypes were as much for the client team as for the consumer, allowing them to live with the brand for a few days and get used to it. The mocked-up ideas were also great to use with prospective customers, who were recruited in small numbers and shown the ideas in an informal setting like a bar or café. Never were they asked whether they liked the name Egg; instead, reactions to the concept were the focus of the research. People loved the brand idea and soon started using the brand name without giving it much thought. Right at the end of the session they were asked what they thought about Egg as a name and some did profess to having been a bit sceptical at the start. However, as it had been presented as a real thing that they could touch and feel they had given it the benefit of the doubt and concentrated on the idea itself. All credit to Prudential for backing the Egg brand: by the end of 2001 it had almost two million customers and had broken even for the first time.

Beyond evaluation to experience

Quantitative testing can play a useful role in brand development when used correctly. It can give a team confidence to back a big idea where the investment stakes are high. However, to ensure that they don't rely on the research to provide the answer on a plate for every initiative, teams need to get beyond evaluation to experience. It is only by launching projects and getting in-market, real-world experience that they can build their own sense of judgement and intuition.

The hit detector

The judges on television talent show *Pop Idol* have a 'nose for a hit'. They always seem to guess correctly which singer the public will vote for. Brand teams need to develop the same kind of intuition and judgement. Sometimes you have to be confident enough about your own belief despite negative test results, especially when working on radical new ideas. This was the case with the successful launch of Flower by Kenzo, which helped boost the brand's sales by 75 per cent in the first six months of 2001. The chairman of parent company LVMH, Bernard Arnault, makes the point as follows:

> When a creative team believes in a product, you have to trust the team's gut instinct. That is the case with a new perfume we launched this year: Flower by Kenzo. We put it forward not because of the tests but because the team believed in it. In the tests people did not know what to make of it – the shape of the bottle is different, and its signature flower is a poppy, which has no scent (2).

Before doing quantitative research, teams need to have a clear point of view about the expected outcome. This is a working hypothesis that can evolve when the results come out but these should tell you 'how high is high', not whether the idea is good or bad. For example, research can be used to help in the process of segmenting a market, by sizing and quantifying the needs of different consumer typologies in a market. However, this is best done when the team already has an idea about the sort of groups it thinks exist and what makes them different. This will help team members analyse the data and explain the results, also giving more colour and depth to the conclusions as a link can be made between the data and real life.

Minimize the downside

In the case of LVMH, Bernard Arnault describes how the downside of a new launch is minimized by producing small volumes at the start of a new introduction. In-market learning is then used to separate winners from losers and modify production quantities accordingly. This is the same approach used by the hugely successful European retailer Zara, as UK managing director Mike Shearwood describes: 'I spend a lot of time in the stores listening to what the customers have told staff. That is the most important part of the job, getting that feedback.' Stocks of undyed fabric and leather are kept on hand at the Spanish factory, minimizing the stock of finished product. New stock of hot items can be made to order and shipped quickly to stores, while less successful lines are not replenished (3).

Although many companies would struggle to match this degree of responsiveness, consumer goods companies doing regional tests have used the principles of minimizing the downside for years. This takes up valuable time and does give the competition the chance to see what you are doing, but at least the learning is based on in-market conditions close to real life. In the past these tests have been in parts of the UK, as was the case with big hits such as Müller yoghurt, Wash & Go shampoo and the drink Bacardi Breezer. In today's more international era the region in question might be a country, with an idea tried out in one place and then quickly exported if it works.

Mining the data

Data mining conjures up images of horribly complex calculations done on huge computers, but it can be much simpler. A favourite example of using data from in-market experience was at Amazon. The new marketing director wanted to stop the practice of sending a present to the top 5000 or so customers as he doubted that the pay-back was sufficient. However, the team doing this activity was sure that it worked and mined the customer data to prove it. They looked at the customers ranked from 4900 to 5000 who got the gift, and compared their buying patterns with customers 5001 to 5100 who just missed out. Increased purchasing after the gifts went out easily paid back the cost of the programme and it was maintained. This simple example shows how teams can be creative in their analysis of in-market experience.

Bring the insight to life

One marketing director described his idea of hell as being 'trapped in an endless Power-point presentation' after sitting through another 100-slide research debrief with a thick, dense report destined for the cupboard. In this approach the real nuggets of insight are not fully exploited, with the time and money spent extracting them going to waste. It's a little like going to the trouble of mining for a rough diamond and then not bothering to trans-form it into the centrepiece of a beautiful piece of jewellery. The challenge of communi-cating insights becomes all the harder once you move beyond the project team to the wider business and senior management.

However, with some effort and money you can bring insights to life in a way that makes them much more striking and inspiring. One excellent way of producing '3D' insights is the increasing use of video to capture consumers using or talking about products. At the simplest level these can be in the form of edited footage from focus groups, although the sound and image quality of this approach leave a great deal to be desired and it can end up being more of a turn-off than a turn-on. A more effective approach is to do specially com-missioned 'vox pop' interviews, where you stop people in the street and ask them pre-prepared questions. The impact of seeing a consumer saying something to camera is so much more powerful than reading it in a research report.

One marketing director told me the story of where such an approach created a break-through on an innovation project in the laundry cleaning arena. He and the brand team passionately believed that delivering washing powder in tablet form was a big idea, much stronger than the planned route of using a cloth bag that would open in the wash. How-ever, there was so much momentum behind the bag idea that the brand team felt it was like banging your head against a brick wall. Consumer data and test results failed to move the senior management, who had invested too much time and money in the other direction and were worried about delaying the launch. As a last resort, the brand team members got together a group of consumers to work with them over a couple of days creating new product ideas and ended up with a shortlist. For all but one of the consumers, the tablet idea was by far their preferred concept. The team asked these enthusiasts to talk to camera and tell the senior managers 'back at the ranch' what they thought. The video footage was used in a last-ditch attempt to convince the board that the tablet concept had more potential than the bag and helped the brand team win the day.

An even more challenging audience for communication of consumer insights was to be found in the designers at Levi's. Added Value insight work threw up many interesting and useful findings, but the team was unsure about how to communicate the results to the designers, who would run a mile from any research that tried to tell them what to do. The solution was to develop a style magazine that looked more like *The Face* than a research debrief, with time spent on copywriting and art direction so it really did resemble the real thing. This quickly became required reading for everyone at Levi's and the European president made it clear that everyone should have one in their briefcase or rucksack.

 ## Key takeouts

1 True insight about consumers, brands and markets can help inspire and inform teams in their search for growth.
2 However, research can only get you so far and it can stifle innovation, waste money and time and be used in place of intuition and judgement.
3 Teams should get beyond exploration to empathy by immersing themselves in the consumer's world. They should also move past evaluation to experience by relying less on testing and more on launching and learning.

 ## 3-part action plan

Tomorrow

Review the research that you plan to do in the coming months. Is it helping uncover deep and meaningful truths about consumers, brands and markets? Or is it being used as a prop to help make marketing decisions that could be made by employing judgement? Are you in danger of killing any new innovation ideas by failing to do them justice in the way they are presented?

This month

Review the current insight foundations that you have for your brand. Are these vivid and rich and do they reflect consumer empathy, not just consumer understanding? Ensure that the insights have been brought to life in 3D so that they inspire and guide people in the business team.

This year

Look at the team of people working on your brand or in your department and ask how close they are to the consumer and brand. Do they have a genuine interest in the category like people at Nike or are they dispassionate observers? To be really challenging, consider yourself as well in this: are you working on a brand or business that you can easily relate to and ideally use yourself? Seek to hire people or recruit people internally who share the same profile as your target user and make the most of their insights and ideas. Ensure that where possible the key agency people, especially creatives, are as close as possible to being consumers of the brand so that they can build real empathy.

Handover

We have now looked at the two key steps to building a solid foundation on which brand strategy work can begin. 'Get real' showed how strategy needs to be linked to actions that generate growth. 'Search for true insight' has suggested ways of getting deep, rich insights about consumers, brands and markets without blowing too much of your marketing budget. Part III will take us on to three pillars of brand strategy. Workout Three, 'Do fewer things, better', looks at how focusing the brand portfolio can boost return on investment. 'Bring your vision to life' then shows how to develop an ambitious vision for each of the brands on which the team decides to focus. The final Workout of Part III, 'Keep the brand on track', addresses the need for a competitive and coherent positioning to help develop a mix that moves the brand towards this vision.

BRAND STRATEGY

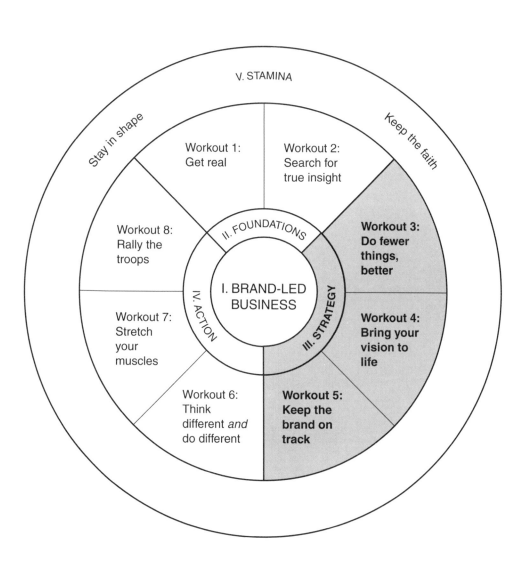

Workout Three:
Do fewer things, better

CHAPTER 4

'Sacrifice plus sweat = success.'

Charlie Finlay

 Headlines

Having too many brands fragments financial and human resources, spreading them too thinly. Winning teams drive profitable growth by being ruthless about identifying and then backing those brands with the best potential to create growth. They focus budgets, energy and commitment and so boost return on brand investment. The key to developing the right portfolio is balancing how many brands you *need* to achieve your business ambitions against how many brands you can afford to *feed* with the available budget.

Many of the success stories from the research for this book had at their heart a new leadership team who focused their team's efforts to boost performance. They often inherited a business where the problem of spreading resources across too many brands had been reinforced by the brand management system itself. Having a dedicated manager to fight each brand's cause actually promoted overenthusiasm for all brands, even those with limited potential. This meant that some weak brands were getting a valuable share of the budget that could have been better spent elsewhere. It was as if every brand was a child needing feeding and if it was not supported it was being starved to death.

We will start by looking at just how much opportunity and need there are for brand focus in the overcrowded and overbranded world we live in, before reviewing the different portfolio strategies that can be used. The Workout will end with a practical, market-driven approach to portfolio planning that can help you do fewer things and do them better.

Fragmentation is bad

Business has clearly got the branding bug big time, to the point where people are suffering from brand overload and the concept of branding is in danger of being devalued. The 'outside-in' thinking described in Chapter 1 can fool companies into thinking that anything with a clever name and fancy logo deserves to be called a brand and supported like one. This has led to a plethora of 'brand wannabes' that lack the strength of reputation and personality to be brands in a true sense. The problem of 'overbranding' has been made worse by the bad habit of always creating a new brand each time a new product concept is created, rather than extending existing brands.

Having, or at least thinking that you have, too many brands is simply bad for business, as it fragments investment and resources. When a company starts considering a product or service as a brand, it tends to provide a team to manage the brand and its own dedicated marketing support. This sucks in not only money but also, just as importantly, management time for briefings, business reviews and approval of marketing activity. This was the case with Midland Bank's ill-fated attempt to create a portfolio of three different product brands in the 1980s. Orchard, Vector and Merridean were targeted at different types of people, with Midland Bank relegated to the role of an endorser. So, for example, if you were the young, thrusting and ambitious type then Vector (from Midland) was the brand for you. Each brand was advertised and in theory this better targeting and adaptation of the product would lead to increased share. However, the investment did not pay back sufficiently and Orchard, Vector and Merridean soon disappeared, never to be seen again. It was one thing to create three names, logos and advertising campaigns, but another altogether truly to build a distinctive promise and personality for each brand.

This case illustrates the need for discipline in creating as few new brands as possible and concentrating efforts on this focused portfolio. Pressing the new brand button is only justified when the stretch from the core brand is so big that the new product or service will lack credibility without a new name. In particular, a new brand may be needed where the price position and/or personality of the new offer is very far from the current position. In the Midland example the stretch from the core to the three product areas was not enough to require the creation of new brands. Simple descriptive names such as 'Saver' and 'Investor' could have been used to explain the different product packages. In contrast, Toyota would have struggled to stretch into the luxury car market, as it lacked exclusivity and prestige. This led to the creation of the Lexus brand to attack this market opportunity.

Even when the stretch from where the brand is today is quite far, there needs to be careful consideration before you give up and create a new brand. This situation came up when working with one of the world's leading mobile communication companies, which wanted to increase its share of the all-important youth market. Its core brand had strong business associations, resulting in an image that was conservative and even somewhat dull. A little bit of branding anarchy started to break out in response to this issue in a couple of smaller markets that were off the radar screen of the global brand team. These markets created their own stand-alone new brands with a different look and feel, which was judged to meet the needs of young people better. In came black, silver and chrome and edgy advertising and out went the corporate colours of the main brand, not even present as an endorser. There was no shortage of creativity and innovation, but this strategy was a trap with several major risks.

First, the creation of a new brand would divert valuable resources and support from the main brand, including probably the youngest, most dynamic people in the brand team. More importantly, the local companies were removing from the main brand one of its best chances to rejuvenate itself by appealing to younger consumers. How could the main brand have any chance of attracting the next generation of users if all the efforts towards this audience were diverted into a new brand? The company decided that a better approach was to refresh and reinvigorate the main brand, including extension into new services and products for younger people. They even found that business people reacted positively to the brand being a little more contemporary and energetic.

Focus is good

Several factors have given companies a wake-up call as we start the new millennium, leading to an overdue focusing of brand portfolios (Figure 4.1). *Growing pressure from the stock market for financial returns* has led to a healthy and long overdue focus on doing fewer things better. As more companies have started to go public with their brand focus efforts, there is growing 'peer pressure' for other companies to follow suit. In addition, *the continual consolidation of the retail sector*, in groceries but also in other markets such as mobile phones, means that bigger brands have better bargaining power to keep their share of shelf space. *The rising cost of media* is also making it more and more expensive to support brands fully. Finally, *mergers and acquisitions* have led to overcrowded brand portfolios that need to be rationalized for financial reasons or because of demands from competition authorities.

Unilever is one of the best publicized examples of brand focus, with a commitment made to cut its portfolio from 1600 to 400 brands, and within this to focus on a core of 40. As Chairman Niall Fitzgerald says: 'Instead of fragmenting resources we are able to invest

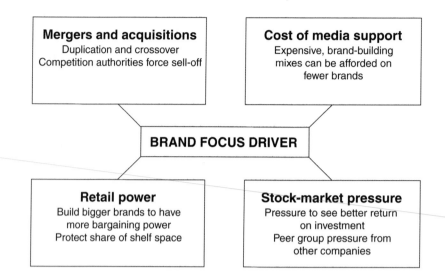

Figure 4.1: Forces driving brand focus.

in significant brand development and big-hit innovation for one or two. We are already seeing the consequences in the performance of our leading brands' (1).

In the case of Unilever, as well as many other companies, a promotion of local autonomy led to the creation of multiple brands *across markets*, with countries often creating their own names, products and packaging. In dandruff shampoo Unilever ended up with Clinic in France, All Clear in the UK, Clear in Italy and Linic in Portugal. In contrast, P&G had the advantage of selling Head & Shoulders dandruff shampoo everywhere from Bombay to Birmingham. This issue is being addressed by harmonizing names and identities over markets, such as renaming Jif as Cif in the UK

The need for focus also exists *within markets*, where multiple brands have often been created to meet each new consumer need that is attacked. In many of these cases a brand extension might have done the job as well but with less investment support. To re-focus the portfolio, weaker brands are being culled and their products 'migrated' to stronger brands. This has led to the disappearance of Radion (now a Sunfresh variant of Surf) and Delight (now part of Flora).

The billion-dollar brand club

The momentum in companies such as Unilever towards focusing on fewer, bigger global brands appears to be unstoppable. The biggest, most powerful brands like Dove, Lipton and Knorr are billion-dollar businesses. A strong core of functional credentials plus rich emotional values allows them to have a large 'footprint' that spans different product sectors. Globally harmonized product design, formulation, packaging and communication produce lower costs but also quicker roll-out of new ideas and products. The term *'megabrand'* can be used as shorthand to describe this sort of brand, which exhibits three characteristics: scale, geographic spread and product stretch (Figure 4.2).

The benefits of brand focus go beyond mere cost reduction to include the stimulation of innovation and creativity. It is good to be one of the focus brands in a portfolio, but if the 'tail' of weaker brands is being cut then growth has to come from one place, and that is you. This is driving a much more aggressive and business-focused approach to accelerate growth on brands like Dove. Whereas the brand purists of the past wanted to restrict Dove to its historical area of expertise in skin cleansing, the brand has been successfully extended into areas such as deodorant and now shampoo. As another example, only a few years ago Magnum mainly launched variants that conformed with the product's history (big, chocolate, ice cream, indulgent, on a stick, for individuals only). However, it is now seen as a brand with huge potential for growth that can be stretched much further. A more disciplined list of 'non-negotiable' equities has helped stimulate innovation such as Magnum Snacksize and Magnum After-Dinner. The opposite extreme of overextension obviously needs be avoided and we will return to this issue in the Workout 'Stretch your muscles'.

The other good news is that contrary to what critics of global branding would have us

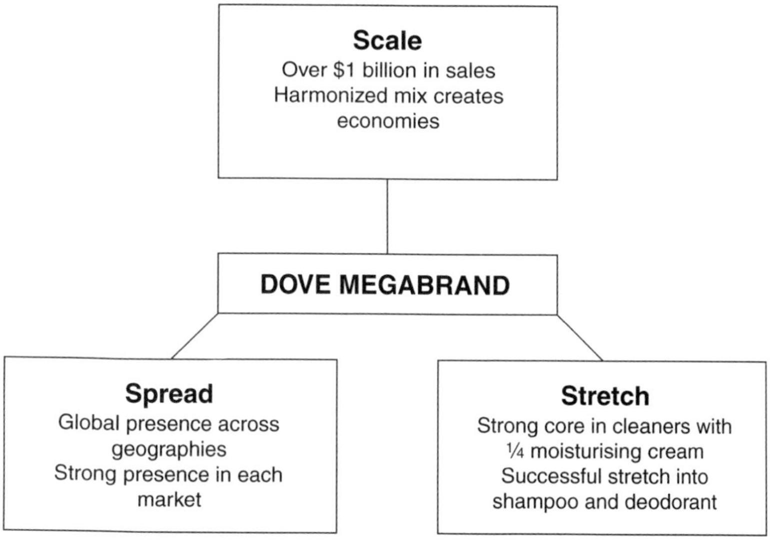

Figure 4.2: The three Ss of megabrands.

believe, the business advantages of harmonization can be achieved with little to no loss on the side of the consumer. Many of the local differences that do exist on brands have no real reason to exist any more, being minor tweaks and changes put in place by local managers adding their own personal touch. Does a consumer in the UK really give a jot whether their cleaner is called Jif or Cif? As long as it still does the job at the same price, they will happily keep buying it.

The Orange France story

In 2001 France Télécom made a bold branding move that dramatically illustrates the concept of brand focus. On June 21 it replaced three mobile network 'product brands' – Itineris (subscription), Ola (pay as you go) and Mobicarte (pay as you go for youth) – with Orange (Figure 4.3). For example, Mobicarte had been managed and supported as a brand in its own right but was relegated to its rightful place as a product descriptor. The re-branding was based on a belief that Orange possessed strong enough functional and emotional values to have a large 'footprint' covering a range of product areas. In addition, the move was driven by a desire to have a single, global mobile brand with nothing in the original portfolio up to this challenge. The re-branding of Itineris, Mobicarte and Ola as Orange was a mammoth task, with 14 million subscribers to inform and retain on Itineris alone. A total of 18 different letters were sent to subscribers to personalize the message depending on the type of contract held, with the top 1000 customers called personally. There was also a need to communicate to a wider audience to build awareness of the Orange brand among potential new users and to reassure the financial community. A $15 million

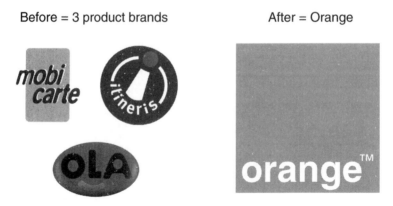

Figure 4.3: Orange France re-branding.

Logos for Itineris, Mobicarte, Ola and Orange reproduced by permission of Orange France.

advertising campaign was used to get across the new message of '*Le future. Vous l'aimez comment?*' (What sort of future would you like?). In addition, a further $15 million was needed for the huge job of re-branding all the promotional, display and retail materials (2). So, was all this money worth it?

There are some major advantages coming out of the focused, mono-brand portfolio. First, there is now only one true brand that needs to be built and maintained. It is much cheaper to invest in creating and enhancing the emotional values and personality of Orange and communicate different product offers underneath it, rather than building three separate stand-alone brands. By advertising one brand not three, the opportunities for savings are considerable. France Télécom spent $140 million on advertising for its mobile division in 2000 alone, so a 20 per cent saving would pay back the re-branding investment in one year. Secondly, over time there are significant savings to be made producing creative work such as websites, signage, advertising and promotional materials. Finally, there are big potential economies of scale from being part of a global marketing offensive on the Orange brand rather than a local operator.

 5-minute workout

What opportunities do you have to 'do an Orange' to your brand portfolio? Do you have any 'brands' like Mobicarte that are really products dressed up in brand clothing? Which brands are strong enough to take up the products or services currently marketed under other, weaker brands?

Different portfolio models

Building the right brand portfolio is about determining the optimum number and deployment of brands in order to maximize profitable growth. This is in essence a trade-off between two factors (Figure 4.4). The first issue is *how many brands you need* to fulfil your

Figure 4.4: Issues driving portfolio strategy.

ambitions. A niche player like auto manufacturer Porsche can grow successfully with a single brand to support its product range. Different cars are designed to target different sectors, but they share similar emotional values and personality and tend to have descriptors such as 911 and 944. In contrast, to cover all segments and value positionings, Ford has used sub-brands like the Fiesta, Ka and Cougar. It has also acquired prestige brands such as Volvo, Aston Martin and Jaguar to stretch further up market than the Ford brand could go. The second issue is *how many brands you can feed* with marketing support and still make a decent return on investment. The need to maximize financial returns will drive you towards as few brands as possible, given the huge cost of developing, launching and sustaining them.

To keep things simple we will consider three main types of portfolio model, mono-brand, sub-brand and multi-brand (Table 4.1), which can result from answering the 'need' and 'feed' questions. Consider reviewing this table first to check out which of the models is most relevant to your case.

Mono-brand

The most cost-effective portfolio for a given market should be a single, powerful brand with a big footprint, such as Orange. As we have seen, factors such as retailer power and rising media costs mean that creating and growing brands is increasingly difficult and expensive. Therefore, there are huge benefits to be obtained from focusing the organization's efforts behind one brand, with simple descriptors used for range navigation. Many of the successful new-economy brands such as Yahoo!, Amazon and Egg have adopted this approach, with a single brand used to market a very wide range of different services (Figure 4.5).

In this model, brand positioning is fundamentally the same across product platforms with a common visual identity and selling line (e.g. 'The future's bright. The future's Orange'). Small differences in competitive environment and core consumer target mean that the benefits and reasons to believe may be tweaked, but the promise, personality and values are the same. The X5, BMW's entry into the off-road market, needed some specific features, such as 4x4 traction and high ground clearance. However, it still looked, felt and drove like 'the ultimate driving machine' in its category. Investment is used to promote awareness of the X5, but this is done with a campaign that has a minimalist, aspirational, BMW house style.

The issue with this approach is that it can restrict the ability of each product to compete fully with more focused competitors. A limited amount of product-specific communication is possible in a brand-based campaign. For example, Virgin tried and failed to enter

Table 4.1: Different portfolio models

	Mono-brand (BMW)	Sub-brand (Gillette)	Multi-brand (P&G's Pantene, Wash & Go and Head & Shoulders)
Band positioning	Consistent across platforms. Small differences in competition, reasons to believe, benefits	Essence, values and core promise consistent. Differences in personality and price positioning	Different by brand platform
Selling line, brand properties (e.g. mnemonics, visual equities)	Common across platforms ('Ultimate Driving Machine')	Common across platforms (The 'best a man can get')	Different by brand
Investment support	Brand campaign used to promote specific product platforms	Sub-brand campaigns used with unifying family feel and tone	Major, dedicated support for each purchase brand
Role of brand support for each platform	Promote awareness of the specific product	Create specific value proposition that tells one chapter of an overall brand story	Build distinctive personality and proposition
Benefits	Savings in design, commercial production, brand management. All communication builds one brand	Some savings in design, commercial production, brand management. Target different segments while building core brand equity to some degree	Clear proposition for each platform. All-out effort to target different segments
Issues	Compromises communication of each platform. Dilution of brand image	Risk of sub-brands being treated like stand-alone brands, getting too much support and not building core brand	Needs major investment for each platform. Can fragment resources

egg: | Individual Money Matters

Nothing for months.

Make your friends green with envy. Get 0%, fixed until 1 September 2002, on balance transfers and new purchases, **11.6% APR** (variable)

Get your paws on one ○

Figure 4.5: Example of mono-brand portfolio.

Used with the kind permission of Egg.

the vodka market, as a more specific, targeted proposition was needed to compete against Smirnoff and Absolut. IBM had a good reputation in computer hardware but struggled to compete in software using the IBM name alone. Hence it bought Lotus to get access to that company's Notes brand of groupware products. Also, if too many extensions are launched the equity of the brand can become diluted and weakened.

To ensure product success and avoid equity dilution, extensions need to be in areas where the brand promise and personality add real value and differentiation. Dove has stuck to this principle by going into areas where its mild moisturization benefit offers a real plus, such as deodorant and shampoo.

Sub-brand

When a single brand with descriptive product names cannot stretch to cover the market opportunities identified, the next step should be to consider sub-branding. In this portfolio there is a strong central brand associated with a rich set of functional and emotional benefits. For example, Gillette stands for performance, masculinity and close shaving in the grooming market. Its uses 'sub-brands' like Blue II, Sensor, Sensor Excel and Mach 3 to meet the needs of different segments and, importantly, support different price points

(Figure 4.6). These names have more emotion and personality than descriptors such as one-blade, two-blade and three-blade, but insufficient strength to be brands in their own right. Few men would have forked out £5 or more to buy a new razor simply called 'Mach 3'. However, they were happy to do this for a 'Gillette Mach 3', where the sub-brand works like a new first name with the Gillette family name to create a 'composite brand'.

There is more difference between sub-brands like Mach 3 and Sensor Excel than between the 3 Series and 5 Series in BMW's mono-brand portfolio. The Mach 3 has a different personality, being more advanced and modern than Sensor Excel. It also has its own advertising campaign with a specific message about the three-blade technology that allows you to shave closer with fewer strokes. However, there is a visible house style and unifying elements such as the focus on shaving performance and the 'Best a man can get' end line

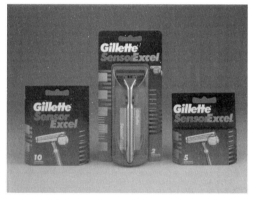
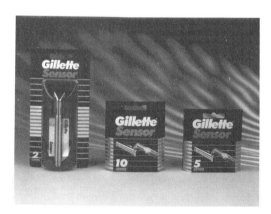
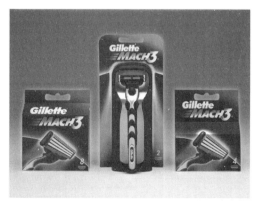

Figure 4.6: Gillette sub-brand portfolio.

Reproduced by permission of The Gillette Company.

and jingle. The Mach 3 proposition tells a new chapter in the Gillette story, but not a different story altogether.

In theory, this approach seems to allow companies to 'have their brand cake and eat it', with savings in brand design and management yet the possibility of a more targeted approach for products. However, in reality it is full of risks and pitfalls and ends up burning a big hole in the pockets of many companies. It is easy to let each sub-brand get too much support, with the budget and resources you would allocate to a true stand-alone brand. When each sub-brand starts to get its own advertising and promotional support, marketing efforts begin to diverge, no longer building and refreshing the core brand idea. This ends up being in effect a 'multi-brand' portfolio and in this case much more support is required for each brand. To be effective, sub-brands need to be clearly 'members of the family' and so require less support than a set of stand-alone brands.

Multi-brand

In this model each brand is targeted against a specific set of needs and consumers and encouraged to fight for itself. The approach allows each brand to be more focused in its proposition and so in theory better meet the needs of its target audience. Each brand has its own distinctive personality, values and promise and needs dedicated support to survive and prosper.

In some cases, for example P&G, brands such as Pantene, Wash & Go and Head & Shoulders stand alone without any meaningful endorsement from the company brand. In other cases an endorser is used to provide extra reassurance. Often the endorser is a company name linked to corporate values, beliefs and competencies, such as the use of Cadbury on chocolate confectionery brands like Fuse, Flake and Double Decker. In the case of Cadbury, significant efforts have been put into creating meaning for the corporate brand through initiatives such as Cadbury World amusement park, Cadbury Café and the sponsorship of television soap opera *Coronation Street*. The Cadbury brand also has many years of heritage behind it. The positive reputation of the brand is shown in *Brand Gym* research done by Taylor Nelson in 2002 with 1000 UK adults, which put it top of a list of nine leading brands rated on delivering against what they promised. An impressive 85 per cent of people thought that Cadbury was good at keeping its promises.

An endorser can truly add value to product brands when it has real equity, as is the case with Cadbury. New products have a better chance of trial as the endorsement reassures you, for example on the quality and taste of the chocolate. However, in some cases logos of faceless companies are simply 'slapped' on the top left-hand corner of a pack and expected to add value. It is unlikely that many people in the UK really care that KitKat is made by Swiss food giant Nestlé and few even spotted the change when this endorsement replaced the old Rowntree name.

The huge downside with a multi-brand portfolio is the cost of supporting several brands. This requires heavy investment in media but also commercial production and design. Even P&G is reviewing its portfolios and looking at cutting down the number of brands. In the UK laundry cleaning market it recently launched a non-biological powder under Ariel, a proposition that had before been offered by the Fairy brand. Time will tell if this is a first move in removing Fairy from the market to allow resources to be focused on the strategically more important Ariel brand.

This section has shown that brand portfolio strategy is less about naming and brand identity and more about how you run your business. Brand bureaucrats make the mistake of thinking that by mimicking the approach of Gillette in design terms they are creating a sub-brand portfolio. However, we have seen that this requires a specific approach to investment and communication strategy. With this in mind, we will now look at how a team can apply the principles of portfolio strategy to its own business by looking at the two critical questions: how many brands you need and how many you can feed.

So, how many brands do *you* need?

A common problem with brand portfolio projects is that managers jump straight into a debate about which brands deserve more or less support, without taking time to look at the bigger picture in a systematic fashion. A better approach is to identify growth opportunities in the marketplace and then consider which of the company's brand assets could be used to attack these. This analysis phase will later inform strategy development, which in turn guides an action plan covering brand issues such as stretch, migration and creation (Figure 4.7).

Growth opportunities

Before you can start to answer the question of how many brands you need, the opportunities for growth have to be identified. This requires the market to be defined and then mapped out.

Defining the market
An important consideration in the mapping process is to define the market as broadly as possible. For example, when segmenting the laundry products category, the major players

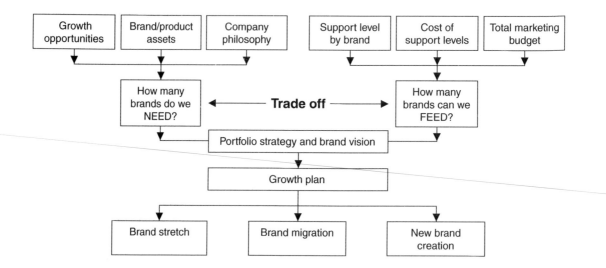

Figure 4.7: Brand portfolio process.

treat cleaning and care as two separate markets and then debate how many brands to have in each. An alternative approach would be to consider these two markets as one and challenge whether all the brands are in fact necessary. Why couldn't Persil, which is strong on both cleaning and care, cover the fabric softener area currently occupied by Comfort? After all, hair-cleaning brands such as Pantene offer conditioners as an integral part of their range. Or think about Coca-Cola. If it had restricted its market definition to its core business of 'colas', rather than a broader definition of 'drinkable refreshment', then it would have missed new opportunities such as sports drinks, fruit juice and water. The broader the market, the more challenging the questions and the bigger the potential savings from rationalization will be.

A sense check does need to be applied when defining the market. In a perfect world any sort of innovation would be up for grabs, even if the company had no ability to make the product in question. However, the reality is that most businesses have a core set of activities for which they have built up both physical and human capital. They are cautious about new areas that require heavy capital investment. For example, Frito-Lay is an expert in salty snacks such as potato and tortilla chips, but it has made limited attempts to diversify into sweet snacks. Understanding the company's capabilities and attitude to capital investment avoids the team running off in directions that have no chance of seeing the light of day.

Mapping the market

Mapping out the market requires different dimensions of segmentation to be considered. One approach is to consider the '6Ps': products, purpose, periods, places, people and price (Figure 4.8). Each of these dimensions can be analysed in turn to identify which are the main drivers of consumer choice and preference. When the driving dimensions have been found, analysis can be focused on understanding them in more detail. For example, in the car market different consumer typologies with different sets of needs and values exist and these groups tend to buy different sorts of car. An office worker with three children living in the town has different needs and attitudes from a retired, well-off couple in the country. A company like Ford can 'anchor' each of its brands on one of these different typologies. For example, Volvo is anchored on urban, professional families concerned about safety and prepared to pay more for it, whereas the Ford brand itself has a more mass-market target.

There are no hard and fast rules about which segmentation variables drive choice between brands, although some general, common-sense guidelines can help. The more emotionally involving a market is, the more important the *people* dimension becomes, especially when the purchase is expensive and visible to others. The watch you wear says something important about who you are, or who you would like to be. In the UK the newspaper you read is an example of a cheaper, daily product that sends an important signal about the sort of

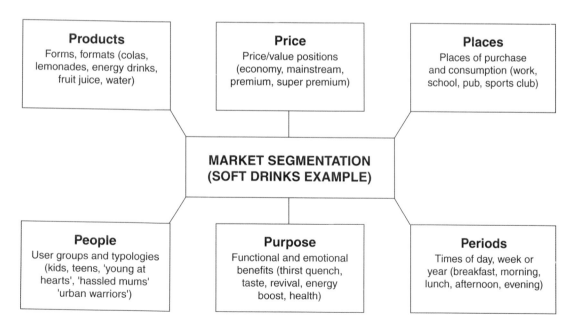

Figure 4.8: Market segmentation example.

person you are. For this kind of market, each of three brands in a portfolio might be positioned against a different consumer typology, with a different bundle of emotional and functional needs. On the other hand, in biscuits the *period* of use is the key driver. There is more difference between one person on different occasions (having a cup of tea alone versus entertaining friends) than between two different people. United Biscuits France has Delacre individual biscuits for everyday drink accompaniment, Delacre Tea Time for inviting guests and BN for children's snack time.

Brand and product assets

Brand assets

The next part of the analysis phase uses a filtering process to identify those brands that can be the pillars of the portfolio and those that should receive reduced support or even be killed. Breaking the definition of a true brand down into a series of filters can help object-ively assess the portfolio: having a name and symbols, being known, being trusted and appealing to head and heart (Figure 4.9). In addition, analysis using the 6 Ps or another framework should be employed to highlight the footprint of the brand: those areas of the market where the brand has a strong presence. For example, in the case of Apple the brand could be anchored on self-expressive creative (*people*) who use computers for work and play (*periods*) and look for ease of use and multimedia connectivity (*purpose*).

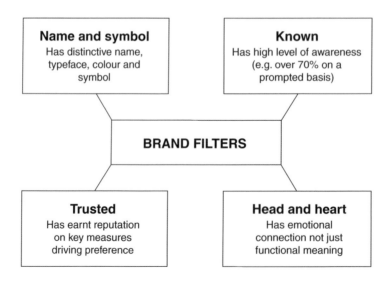

Figure 4.9: Brand asset filters.

This analysis should make use of hard data to measure aspects such as brand awareness and usage plus qualitative work to help uncover brand imagery. For example, France Télécom's mobile brands lacked depth and emotional appeal, especially Mobicarte and Ola. However, the key issue here is not merely what the brands stand for today, but their potential to stretch their footprint and cover new market opportunities. This can be assessed by analysis, looking at whether a brand is linked to one specific format or if it has a richer, broader set of emotional values that could be leveraged into new areas. Also, mocking up ideas for new products is a good way of exploring the issue of stretch, giving useful feedback on the boundaries that consumers put on different brands. The objective here is not to ask *if* a brand could or should launch these products. Rather, the idea is to understand the *degree* of stretch and hence the difficulty of extending the brand.

In a portfolio project for United Biscuits in France, the BN brand seemed to have potential to grow, although it had been underexploited to date. The brand was strongly linked to a square, chocolate-filled biscuit with a smiley face eaten by kids with milk at their 4 pm '*goûter*'. Indeed, the branding on the pack was actually not BN but 'Le BN', further reinforcing the impression that brand and product were one and the same. Qualitative research on the brand had already shown that BN was rich in emotional values like childhood fun, friendliness and play. To explore further the potential of BN, product prototypes were developed to visualize a bigger brand platform, with several new products. For example, one of the new products was based on re-branding Chocland, a pack of small animal-shaped biscuits, as BN-Land. When presented to consumers their reaction was 'About time too!', illustrating that it is often manufacturers' conservatism rather than consumers' resistance that stops brand stretch. The BN brand's equities of goodness, taste appeal and fun were easily stretched into new areas and Chocland was confirmed to be a product descriptor, not a true brand.

Product assets

In addition to understanding the brands in the portfolio, you may also need to assess the potential of different products in the range. For some mono-brand portfolios this is obviously the key issue, as there is only one brand being used across the range. A brand's product or service offer can be thought of as an iceberg made up of multiple layers of products or services (e.g. current account, savings, pensions). The brand team members live, breathe and perhaps even dream about their products so they know them inside out, whereas Joe Public spends a fraction of his day thinking about them. As a result, consumers are only aware of the tip of the brand iceberg, with the rest below the waterline (Figure 4.10).

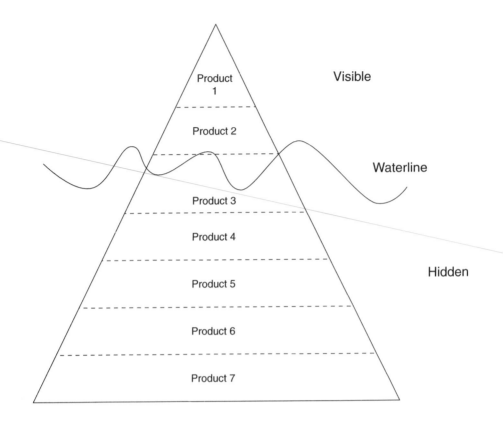

Figure 4.10: The brand iceberg.

Lowering the waterline of visible products is a long, tiring and expensive business, as shown by a research project for an online bank. Customers were asked what sorts of services *they* would be interested in seeing on the site. 'Share dealing would be great,' suggested one. 'And I think they should do insurance,' added another. The client watching the group was by this point holding his head in his hands: the bank already offered all the services that had been suggested, some of which had even been advertised. Developing a product portfolio strategy helped the team decide that too many products were being promoted. Some of these, such as the credit card, were clearly 'star products' at the tip of the iceberg. They had good awareness, did a lot for the brand image and were still attracting new users. Other products such as mortgages had some advertising and promotion, but were far below the waterline of awareness. Getting them on to most consumers' radar screen was prohibitively expensive. The marketing plan was re-worked to put more of the money behind products with real potential for growth. Slowly but surely the waterline dropped and one or two more focus products started to become visible. On other smaller products where funding was reduced, sales kept chugging along at a respectable rate. Rather than starving to death, these products survived on the back of word of mouth and site visitors finding their own way to them.

In the same way that brand assets are critiqued to understand their current strength and future potential, products also need to be reviewed carefully. Which ones have the best potential for growth and deserve to get the bulk of the marketing budget put behind them? Which others should be left to tick along with reduced support and which should be withdrawn? Again, emotions need to be put to one side in objectively analysing product potential. This is hard to do, as certain underperforming products often survive as they are the 'pet project' of someone senior in the business. One trick is to imagine that you are starting from scratch in building a product range. If you could only have one product in your range to cover the maximum number of needs, occasions and consumers, which one would it be? With this core product in place, ask yourself which product you would add next, and justify why it is needed. Continue in this way with the third, fourth and fifth products and you will quickly see which products have a clear role in the portfolio and which are really superfluous. Consider how to reduce the investment of time and money in these peripheral products or how to discontinue them altogether.

Company philosophy

A final factor that may influence the question of how many brands are needed is company philosophy. Whatever the objective and financial arguments, companies may have different points of view about the best portfolio strategy. P&G has been a fervent believer in letting multiple brands fight against themselves for market share, with the corporate name appearing only in small print on the back of the pack. In contrast, L'Oréal makes much more overt use of the company name as an endorser with the well-promoted tagline 'Because I'm worth it'.

Overlap and underlap

The final step in this stage is to bring together the analysis of growth opportunities and brand assets. Specifically, the team needs to see how the existing brand portfolio performs against the key dimensions that drive choice. This should identify three sorts of issues: overlap, underlap and future opportunities.

Overlap is where several brands are going after the same needs or consumers. In this case, some hard questions should be asked about whether the stronger brand couldn't take on products or services currently marketed under other, weaker brands. This was the case with the migration of Delight low-fat spread under Flora. The alternative to brand harmonization is to push brands apart to increase the total footprint of the portfolio. When AOL bought Compuserve and Netscape there was a risk that these three Internet service providers would overlap. To push the brands apart, AOL was managed as the mainstream family brand, Netscape focused on inexperienced surfers looking for a basic service and Compuserve targeted heavy, small and home office users.

Underlap is where none of the brands is fully effective and competition is winning business. The first reaction should be to extend the strongest brand to take up these opportunities, such as Coca-Cola launching Diet Coke for health-conscious consumers and Caffeine-Free for young kids. An opportunity to better meet the needs of families drinking at home led to the larger 1.5l PET bottle. In these cases the stretch was mainly functional and so the Coke brand could extend to meet the new needs credibly. However, if the stretch requires a different set of emotional values a new brand may be needed. Coca-Cola decided that new brands Burn and Bonaqua were required to go after opportunities in energy drinks and bottled water respectively.

Finally, there is a necessity to think to the *future* about new or emerging needs in the market. Unilever strongly believed that weight control was an important and growing requirement and had no brand to meet this, leading to the acquisition of Slimfast. Many innovations come from identifying these sorts of needs and creating an answer to them before the competition.

This analysis phase should have led to the answer to the question: 'How many brands do you need?' The answer should reflect an understanding of the growth opportunities in the market and an objective assessment of which brands are best placed to meet them. In addition, brands that require stretching, creating or killing should have been agreed. The number of brands that the team thinks it needs now must be confronted with the harsh reality of financial returns by asking: 'How many brands can you feed?'

How many brands can you feed?

The question of how many brands a company can afford often seems to be even harder to answer than how many it needs. Big, international companies with talented teams of managers consistently overestimate how many brands they can effectively support. Simple maths can help you avoid making the same mistake.

Cost of support

The first variable to pin down is the cost of supporting a brand in a given market. This figure should be for the total marketing cost including promotions and not just advertising spend. Typically investment levels fall into the following categories:

- Build aggressively: growing share and supporting major new innovations.
- Build: growing volume in line with or just ahead of market growth.
- Maintain: protecting volume but accept some decline.
- Manage for profit: emphasis is on profit generation (sometimes called milking).

The cost of brand support in a market can be worked out using sophisticated analytical techniques and statistical modelling. However, most teams who have experience of working in a market can make a good stab at the cost of supporting a brand.

Brand investment plans

The next piece of the equation is to work out the *planned* level of support for each of the brands in the portfolio. This can first be done by asking each brand team to select the level of support it has in mind for the next year. Invariably, the answers tend to be towards the higher end of 'build' or 'build aggressively', with the odd 'maintain' and no 'manage for profit' in sight. The reasons for this type of answer profile are easy to understand: people have learnt from experience that launching stuff that grows sales and builds share tends to be a better way of getting promoted than managing for profit. It is normal that people who have developed a brand will seek to maximize the support they can get for it. This is why setting the right portfolio strategy requires strong leadership, with a clear focus on the profitable growth of the *total* portfolio at the top of the agenda.

Total marketing budget

The total marketing budget available for the portfolio needs to be established. In most cases there will be a provisional number for this in the three- to five-year plans that companies are normally required to undertake. This figure can be used as a starting point in what is an iterative exercise, with the figure being challenged if the team can show that it can deliver more profit with increased budget.

Budget sense check

With the three data points of cost of support, brand investment plans and total marketing budget established, a simple sense check can then be carried out. The level of support each team has asked for is added up to get a total figure and then compared to the available marketing budget (Table 4.2). From experience, the result tends to be a required budget at least 20–40 per cent bigger than the planned resources. This shortfall is normally addressed by supporting all the brands, but reducing the money given to each. The weaker brands are oversupported and eat up valuable resources. This results in the stronger brands being underfunded and missing out on possible growth opportunities. A better solution is to make tough calls and focus support at decent levels behind the few brands with real potential for growth.

Table 4.2: Budget sense check

	Support level	Cost/year
Brand A	Build aggressively	$15 million
Brand B	Build aggressively	$15 million
Brand C	Build	$10 million
Brand D	Maintain	$5 million
TOTAL SPEND		$45 million
ACTUAL BUDGET		$37 million

So, before you decide that a sub-brand or multi-brand portfolio strategy is the right one for your business, be sure that you have the necessary budget. It is one thing to draw an interesting portfolio model on paper and even design the packs with the sub-brand on them. It is another thing altogether to have deep enough pockets to support this correctly.

Finally, a more fundamental question about the economics of the market itself will also influence how many brands you can support. In a big market where the margins are good there is sufficient total margin available to support a large number of brands. In the UK shampoo market, for example, the leading brand has tended to have less than 15 per cent in volume terms and many brands with much lower shares still make money. In smaller markets or where the industry margins are low, such as in washing powder or toilet tissue, the market can support fewer profitable brands. This means that the decision to launch a new brand rather than extend an existing one is even less likely to be the right strategy.

Setting the right strategy

Following the analysis phase, the two questions of 'need' and 'feed' have to be brought together to define the right portfolio strategy in what is usually an iterative approach. For example, a team may decide that it needs three brands to meet all the growth opportunities but finds that it can only afford two with current budgets. Its members have to go back and challenge the assumption of how many brands they need, or uncover more growth to justify a bigger budget.

A matrix can be used to summarize the portfolio strategy. This captures the anchors for each brand and their investment levels (Table 4.3). Each of the brands in the portfolio also needs a clear vision and positioning. The process of portfolio strategy and brand vision is iterative, as one depends on the other. The role of a brand in the portfolio may be influenced by the vision that the team has for it. On the other hand, the vision for the brand should be guided by the role it should play in the portfolio strategy. In practice you can start in either place, but ensure that the iteration process starts quickly to avoid wasting time on perfecting and crafting either part of the total growth vision. We will look at the issue of brand vision more in the next Workout, 'Bring your vision to life'.

Table 4.3: Brand portfolio summary (simplified)

	Pantene	**Wash & Go**	**Head & Shoulders**
Investment	Build aggressively	Maintain	Build
Products	Shampoo, condition, style	2-in-1 shampoo	Shampoo, lotions
People	Urban women	Families	Men with dandruff
Places	Supermarkets	Supermarkets	Pharmacies
Periods	All occasions	All occasions	Skewed winter
Purpose	Shine, strength	Condition	Dandruff free
Price (Index)	110	100	130
Share of portfolio	40%	30%	30%
Share of investment	60%	10%	30%

Growth plan

With the strategy in place, there is a need to develop a clear action plan for implementing it. This is vital to ensure that the portfolio strategy exercise does not turn into an extended exercise in brand bureaucracy. There are three main thrusts to this action plan, with increasing levels of investment required.

Brand migration

Where a decision has been taken to harmonize brands, a plan is required to re-brand some of the products in the range and attempt to retain the loyal consumers as the change happens. This sort of change is becoming much more common. Although consumers may protest in focus groups when you threaten to change their favourite brand of chocolate or dairy spread, if the change is handled well volumes can normally be maintained. Mars has led the way in re-branding, changing Marathon to Snickers, Happy Dog to Cesar and Opal Fruits to Starburst. The company established a sequence of branding that has become the standard approach to such moves:

- Stage 1: Advance warning (Marathon – about to become Snickers).
- Stage 2: Reminder (Snickers – previously known as Marathon).
- Stage 3: Completion (Snickers).

The amount of time taken for each stage depends on the case, and is influenced by the amount of money spent on communication, the size of the change and the degree of attachment that consumers have to the old name.

Brand stretch

This involves using existing brands to capitalize on new opportunities, avoiding the cost of creating new brands. Done well it can also have a positive effect on the core brand, as long as the new product idea has sufficient appeal and relevance to make a significant impact on the marketplace. A good guideline is that the new launch should be adding about 10 per cent or more in incremental sales to make it interesting. Also, wherever possible new launches should be delivering better gross margins, so that the cannibalization that will inevitably occur at least has a positive effect on the overall profitability of the portfolio. We will return to this issue in the Workout 'Stretch your muscles'.

Brand creation

This should be the last resort after all other avenues have been explored. Creating a new brand is necessary when the stretch required is so far from any of the current brands that a new brand is needed for the new offer to be credible and motivating for consumers.

Key takeouts

1 Fragmentation is bad. It dilutes financial and human resources over too many brands and so reduces return on brand investment.

2 Focus is good. Highlighting the strongest brands and channelling efforts behind them ensures that investment goes against the best opportunities for growth.

3 Developing the right portfolio strategy should be a thorough and analytical process. It should take into account how many brands you really *need* to address the growth opportunities identified and how many you can afford to *feed* with the available funds.

 ## 3-part action plan

Tomorrow

With your team, do a simple version of the exercise on how many brands you can feed. Take your brand portfolio and get each team to suggest the level of support it is planning for its brand. Add these up to calculate how much this would cost for the whole portfolio, and then compare this to your total budget. If the two figures match, you are in the lucky position of having a healthy portfolio. If, as is more likely, there are not enough funds to go around, then start to ask some difficult questions. Which of the brands really have potential to grow and which are weaker and getting more support than they deserve?

This month

Look at the growth opportunities that exist in your market and understand in more detail the brand and product assets that are at your disposal. Where is the underlap where no brand is meeting consumer needs, and where is the overlap where several brands are going after the same opportunity? Commit to cutting support on the weakest 20 per cent of the brand portfolio to free up time, energy and budget on new projects with better growth potential.

This year

Over a period of a year you should work to re-focus your efforts fundamentally, moving from strategy into action. Pay special attention to the structure of the team, as resource and money often get diverted to where people are spending their time. Which brands have the best potential to grow and so deserve more staffing and the attention of your best people? Which other brands should have their teams reduced or even removed altogether? You may be amazed how some products will chug along at a decent rate even when they have less management time spent on them.

 ## Handover

This Workout has emphasized the need to take a disciplined and structured approach to focusing financial and human resources behind the brands that have the best potential for growth. These brands will need to stretch their footprints to cover new segments and markets, possibly taking over products and services from other, weaker brands. The biggest of these brands are likely to be members of the billion-dollar club and global businesses in their own right. In order to inspire and guide the development of these focus brands, the next Workout looks at how you can 'Bring your vision to life' for each of them.

'The problem with not having a goal is that you can spend your life running up and down the pitch and never scoring'.

Bill Copeland

 ## Headlines

Having a vision of what you want to be and where you want to get to can be a powerful source of energy and inspiration. It gives clear direction to the business and adds a sense of purpose to people's work. However, too many visioning exercises become bogged down in time-consuming and expensive processes that end up churning out generic mission statements. These talk about satisfying the holy trinity of shareholders, customers and employees, but in many cases the business itself continues to run as usual. To have impact a vision needs to be more ambitious and must be brought to life by being translated into tangible actions that drive growth.

The winning teams from the research for this book all had a clear vision for their brand and business that inspired and guided them to boost performance and create growth. They were ambitious about their desired destination and how they wanted to get there, not satisfied with the status quo. In contrast, less successful teams were happy to 'truck along' and do business as usual, content if they delivered moderate growth. Without a clear goal to shoot for they lacked the energy and motivation to deliver exceptional results, in the same way that a recreational jogger lacks the commitment of someone training for a marathon.

Further evidence of the importance of vision in driving performance can be found in the extensive research done by Collins and Porras (1). Their six-year research project looked at 18 visionary companies such as 3M and Merck and compared each of them with a similar competitor considered to be good but not great. The stock return of the visionary companies over the period 1926–90 was $6356 compared to $955 for the comparison companies and $415 for the market.

In this Workout we will look at what developing a vision entails, how to ensure it has an impact on the business and how to start your journey.

Where do you want to go today?

In contrast to brand positioning, which is consumer focused, vision is about you and *your* ambitions. It is about where you want to go and the way you want to get there. One manager put it well by saying that it was about 'who we want to be when we grow up'. There are four key components necessary when developing a vision: purpose, destination, values and strategic thrusts (Figure 5.1). While these can be applied at different organizational levels, from a whole company to a business unit or category, we will focus on their use in defining brand vision. This applies most obviously to corporate mono-brands such

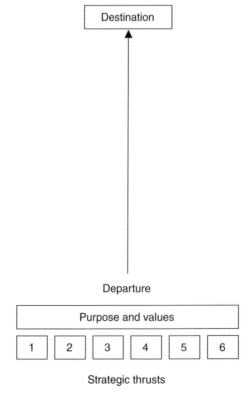

Figure 5.1: The components of brand vision.

as Starbucks and Amazon. However, the principles can equally be applied to give a sense of direction and ambition to major product brands such as Dove or Lipton, which are after all global billion-dollar businesses in their own right.

Purpose (or mission)

The purpose defines the reason for the brand to exist beyond the purely financial. The purpose should capture a higher-level, more emotionally driven concept about the role that the brand seeks to play in improving everyday life, however modest. For example, the purpose of the pharmaceutical company Merck is 'preserving and improving human life'.

Getting clarity on purpose is not merely an intellectual exercise and has several concrete benefits. First, it gives a greater sense of meaning to the work that people do on a brand, making them more motivated and committed. There are many companies where asking the purpose of the business will get not much more than 'creating shareholder value' in response. However, people working for businesses like Merck where work has a meaning beyond the purely financial tend to deliver better results. To refer again to the work of Collins and Porras, they say:

> Profitability is a necessary condition for existence and a means to more important ends, but it is not the end itself for many of the visionary companies. Profit is like oxygen, food, water and blood for the body; they are not the *point* of life, but without them, there is no life.

The other main benefit of clarifying brand purpose is that it can stimulate you to have a broader and more inspiring definition of the market you are trying to serve. Blockbuster saw itself for a long time as being in the 'video rental' business, a functional and quite limited market definition. Today its purpose is closer to 'making a night in as entertaining as a night out' and it refers to itself as a 'home entertainment' business. This broader, more emotionally driven purpose is reflected in the much wider range of products and services that Blockbuster now proposes. It rents out video games and DVDs in addition to videos and sells some of the other things needed to enjoy a night in, such as popcorn, soft drinks and ice cream. It also proposes other supporting services, such as an online guide to find films you will like and a monthly movie magazine.

Destination

Destination is about setting an ambitious 5–10-year target that the brand wants to achieve. This should be stretching in order to challenge the team to think of big, bold initiatives to create growth. The objective is to push yourself to think about how big and successful you could be if you truly fulfilled your potential. As Mark Luce, now Managing Director of beer company Pilsner Urquell, says: 'If you are going to climb a mountain, you might as well go for Everest, not a walk in the Yorkshire Dales.'

It is often helpful to have a financial component to the destination as it gives an idea of stretch. In the case of Pilsner Urquell, now part of South African Breweries (SAB), the destination is 'To be a top 5 international beer brand within 5–10 years'. This will mean a tenfold increase in sales volume, showing how big SAB's ambitions are for the brand, until now strong only in its home market of the Czech Republic. In another example, when starting Amazon Jeff Bezos had a clear idea of his desired destination: to become the biggest bookstore on earth. After several years of rapid growth bringing this destination closer, a new milestone was set. Bezos directed the company towards breaking even by the end of 2001, quite a challenge given the hundreds of millions of dollars in losses that it had already clocked up. However, this stretchy target mobilized the entire business and forced people to find radical improvements in efficiency to boost return on brand investment. The target was delivered on time.

Values

Values are the principles and beliefs that guide the way team members work together. Their concrete application should be visible in the day-to-day working practices of the business. It is best to limit them to no more than five or six in number to make them easy to remember and implement. Where possible you should be brave and bold enough to make the brand values distinctive and even provocative. It is easy to end up with a set of standard vision words such as 'respect', 'diversity' and 'excellence'. Contrast these words with the value of 'No politics, no bullshit' that one managing director was ballsy enough to have in a vision statement. It sent a clear signal about the sort of open and direct culture that he was looking for. He was also determined to ensure that all the bits of the vision passed the 'pub test': he wanted to be confident of explaining the vision to a colleague over a beer without it feeling artificial.

Thrusts

These are the key strategic initiatives that help drive the team towards its destination and are typically five to six in number. The thrusts are perhaps the most important part of the visioning process as they contain the tangible projects that translate the vision into action.

Each thrust has an overall theme, such as 'Step-changing our success in new product development'. A limited number of work streams then detail how the thrust will be implemented. Inspired and guided by the brand purpose, the thrusts propel the team towards its destination on what we can think of as the 'journey'. This is shown on Figure 5.1 as a straight line, which is of course not realistic. No team, however great, manages to get from start to end without going off course a few times. The key to success is knowing that you are going off course quickly and being able to navigate your way back on course. We will come back to this issue in the next Workout, 'Keep the brand on track'.

Putting the pieces together: Ben & Jerry's

The way the building blocks of the visioning process work together are shown in an example for Ben & Jerry's in Table 5.1. This is based on literature on the firm (2) plus a

Table 5.1: Vision for Ben & Jerry's

Purpose
To make, distribute and sell the finest-quality product while operating the company in a way that actively recognizes the central role that business plays in society. To initiate innovative ways to improve the quality of life of the local, national and international communities. At the same time, to operate the company on a sound fiscal basis of profitable growth.

Destination (five years)
To double the size of the Ben & Jerry's brand to make it a key part of Unilever's ice-cream business, by extending geographic scope and product stretch, while staying true to the founding values and mission.

Values (and implications)
Sharing success: continue profit share programme and policy of promotion from within

Activism: continue with local, national programmes and start one major international programme.

Fun: spread the Ben & Jerry's spirit of work hard, play hard; as we expand select Unilever transfers on basis of fit with values to 'maintain the magic'.

Thrusts
1 *Innovation*: stretch into frozen desserts and toppings kits.
2 *Geographic expansion*: focus on securing the UK and French positions, building southern Europe and Scandinavia and entering Asia.
3 *Culture*: protect the culture of the company as we become part of the Unilever business, proactively seek to share and take on board learning.
4 *Advertising*: invest more aggressively in above-the-line support behind communication that has a step change in effectiveness, learning from Unilever's best practice.
5 *Supply chain*: stay loyal to our values-led sourcing while taking on board manufacturing know-how to cut cost of goods to re-invest in the brand.

---

guess at how the vision might have been modified following the acquisition of the brand by Unilever.

The company clearly sees its *purpose* as including but going way beyond the normal aspects of product quality and financial returns, to cover making a real impact on the community. This sense of purpose informs everything from sourcing milk from Vermont cow farmers who are under threat of bankruptcy, to encouraging staff to spend time helping out with worthy causes. The *destination* is to grow the business dramatically through geographical and product stretch, while protecting the values and mission. The *values* clearly do guide the way the company is run and the founders even called their approach to managing the business 'values-led'. Values such as caring for the community are integrated into the fabric of the business, not merely tacked on the side like a plaster, as happens with many social and corporate responsibility initiatives. The *thrusts* again reflect a desire to build the business while staying true to the spirit of the company and its roots as a 'cause-driven' company.

Just another frame on the wall

Vision can be a potent stimulus for growth when it captures the destination, values and thrusts of a bunch of ambitious people. However, as with all brand strategy, there is always the risk that brand bureaucracy will take over and reduce the business impact of the process. Some of the risks to avoid include using an off-the-shelf strategy, not walking the talk and wordsmithing.

Off-the-shelf strategy

Take a look at many mission and vision statements and you will see that they are the same. They offer praise to the holy trinity of business, espousing the desire to 'meet and excel customer needs', 'produce exceptional returns for shareholders' and 'harness the talent of our people'. Hamel and Prahalad put it well by saying:

> In fact, if we took the mission statements of 100 large industrial companies, mixed them up while everyone was asleep, and reassigned them at random, would anyone wake up tomorrow morning and cry, 'My gosh, where has our mission statement gone?'

They talk of the need to offer team members 'the enticing spectacle of a new destination' that gets beyond the generic, cookie-cutter strategies used by so many companies (3). For example, Blockbuster's purpose of 'Making a night in as entertaining as a night out' is specific to the company and requires stretch way beyond simply renting videotapes to be fulfilled.

 ## 5-minute workout

Get out the vision and mission for your brand and cross out the three generic statements about customers, employees and shareholders. Is there anything left, or do you now have a content-free vision? Any company failing to do these basics will obviously not stay in business for long, but they alone are not a vision for your business. You need to come up with something different or at least give a twist to the basic statements.

Not walking the talk

Many companies have spent a fortune developing vision and mission statements that proudly adorn the walls of plush receptions. However, behind the scenes it is 'business as usual' with no tangible change at all. For the vision to have any impact people should see it in action as a living, breathing thing, not a fancy piece of paper in a posh frame. Indeed, the vision should almost not need to be written down if it is interwoven into the fabric of the business. Nike's passion for sport is visible in the hiring of people who share this passion and a campus that includes amazing sports facilities for employees.

Wordsmithing

Another, even bigger problem is that like so much of strategy, visioning exercises can fall into the 'pyramid polishing' trap that we saw in the 'Get real' Workout: box filling and wordsmithing rather than focusing on the ambition and actions that this implies. Hiring a bunch of expensive management consultants risks adding several zeros to the budget and several months to the timeline, with a limited chance of producing more impact on the business. This brings us to the subject of picking the right team and process to develop a brand vision.

Starting your journey

Bringing to life a vision for your brand that helps drive growth does not require a complex process run by an army of consultants. What it does need is a small team of smart and motivated people challenging themselves to answer some tough questions.

Right people

As with all of the Workouts in *The Brand Gym*, success in visioning starts and ends with people. Process and tools can help the right team capture, structure and bring to life their ideas about where to take the brand and the business. However, no process will deliver a big and stretchy ambition for a brand if you do not have a bunch of ambitious people working on it. In some cases the leader of the brand will set the vision in an autocratic fashion and the rest of the team has to jump on board. This is particularly the case for monolithic corporate brands where the CEO is also the founder. Howard Schultz is still the chairman of Starbucks but he is also the 'chief global strategist', making it clear how involved he remains in setting the vision and driving people towards it. The success of his approach cannot be challenged when you consider the explosive growth of the Starbucks brand over the last decade (Figure 5.2) (4).

However, in many cases the leader will opt for a more participative approach. In this case, care should be taken to select a small group of smart and ambitious managers, as this is more likely to produce a distinctive strategy and also save time. The rest of the business can then be involved in developing action plans that help get the brand towards its destination. In contrast, the bottom-up approach practised by some companies takes months or

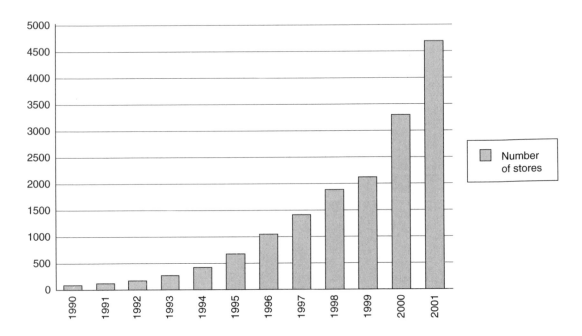

Figure 5.2: Growth in Starbuck's outlets.

even years to consult everyone on what direction the brand should adopt. This is a little like the captain of a ship asking all hundred crewmembers and a few passengers about the best way to head the boat. By the time a direction has been agreed, the ship is too far off course ever to arrive safely at its destination and may even have been holed by a nasty iceberg.

Right deadline

Many visioning exercises take far too long, eating up months and even years of management time. During this extended period of introspection the brand and business are continuing to head on their old course, potentially veering further and further away from the direction they need to take. It is important to remember that all a visioning process can do is capture, structure and bring to life the ambitions and dreams of a group of people. If the raw material is there in the team, then the ideas will come out quickly and relatively easily. However, no length of time will be sufficient for a group of average performers to develop an inspiring and compelling vision.

An example of just how quickly a team can start implementing a vision came on a project with the UK directors of Blockbuster. They developed a new vision for their business that required a radical change in the level of service given, especially for existing customers. One concrete idea suggested was offering an 'amnesty' to people who owed a small amount of money and as a result had not come back out of embarrassment. This was potentially a huge pool of dormant members who could be re-activated. The team agreed that stores would phone these customers and offer them the chance to come in and rent a film for free, with the debt written off. How long would your company take to agree and implement such an idea? A couple of months? A few weeks? The Blockbuster team went ahead and did it *that weekend*.

A visioning team should have a tight deadline and a clear brief to translate the vision quickly into concrete actions that can have a positive business impact. The process should typically have the three main stages detailed below.

1 *Ignition.* This session should be a high-energy, exciting and refreshing one to create the destination, purpose and thrusts. Think carefully when selecting the venue so that you have one that breaks the mould of the corporate meeting room and inspires the team. Try to get a venue in line with the spirit of the workshop, such as the Design Museum if there is an emphasis on creativity, or a sporting setting if the focus is on performance.

2 *Launchpad.* A couple of weeks later you can share with the team a finalized version of the vision, which you will have been discussing and refining since the first workshop. Then

the focus should be on action, working to flesh out each of the strategic thrusts and agree detailed action plans, responsibilities and timings. At the end of the project with Blockbuster, the team wound up with a huge handwritten flowchart on one wall that had all the key programmes of work for the next two to three years. It was a huge help for the team to see how all the work streams fitted together and built towards the destination. After this event work should start in earnest on each thrust that brings the vision to life.

3 *Progress*. About three months is a good amount of time to leave between the launchpad workshop and a first formal progress meeting. It is a chance to see how people have moved ahead against the thrusts, and spend some time working on one or two of them as a team. Try to avoid the session becoming merely another bored board meeting, nevertheless. Keep the spirit of the vision alive by having a theme inspired by the purpose and choose a venue that fits. Make sure that some early 'quick wins' are shared to show the team how the vision is being implemented and generating early signs of growth. It is important at this stage to keep up momentum and stop people falling back into the old ways of working.

Right process

The design of a visioning process needs to deliver against two main objectives. First, it should challenge the team to be as ambitious as possible and fully explore the potential of the brand for growth. To do this exercises will be required to provide external examples of success to stimulate new thinking and expand the brand boundaries. In addition, the team should be projected into the future and then asked to work back to reality in order to get the right degree of stretch and not be overly constrained by the current situation. Secondly, the process needs to ensure that the team moves from vision into action, working on the thrusts that will drive it towards the vision. Actions that can be implemented immediately should be part of this work to allow the team to start bringing the vision to life straight away.

Most teams find it helpful to have a facilitator to help design the process and run the key workshops. You can do everything by yourself, but it is hard to be an active team member and at the same time have responsibility for running the process. Also, an external partner helps bring a fresh perspective. They have no vested interest in the business so they are more able to challenge the current business model and push the team to consider new ideas. The facilitator can be a consultant from the outside or an expert from within the company who works in a different part of the business.

A number of exercises that have been 'road tested' on visioning projects are detailed below. If you do not need to work on a detailed visioning process at the moment you may want to skip ahead to the end of this chapter.

Heaven and hell

This exercise is usually a real wake-up call for the team working on the vision. You simply ask each person to think about the project at hand and then note down what heaven would be like and what hell would be like. These can be ideas to do with the outcome of the project, but also the process of doing it. Having done this a few times, a similar set of answers tend to come up (Table 5.2).

You can start to see the pattern. All the stuff under Heaven is externally focused on beating the competition and exciting consumers, whereas all the stuff on the right is to do with internal politics and inertia. This sort of outcome encourages teams to start addressing the internal issues by choosing to work differently as a team. They might not be able to change the way the whole company works overnight, but they can decide to change their own working processes. Also, the Heaven summary is a great reminder to keep coming back to if the discussion starts to get bogged down in internal, intricate details.

Table 5.2: Answers to heaven and hell exercise

Heaven	Hell
• Building market share	• Internal arguments and politics
• Fantastic ads I'm proud of	• Being trapped in Powerpoint
• People want to work with us	• No money to do what we want
• Consumers talk about us	• All talk and no action, again!

A fresh start: Newco

It is very hard for people not to bring their day jobs into a visioning process and see the problem in the context of their local business. People may say, 'In Germany we tried that and it failed.' Or 'In Latin America the brand is much newer and we could never sell these sort of products.' However, for a successful vision-building exercise you do need your team members to focus on their role as part of the strategic task and not their role as a local or regional representative. They have been selected for the process because of their talent and expertise, not just for their experience in a part of the world. An exercise to shake things up a bit can help get people out of their normal roles.

After a break in the day, say that some bad news and some good news has arrived from head office. The bad news is that the business is being closed down and the whole team has been made redundant. (It's a little worrying when most people in the meeting look happy at this prospect!) The good news is that the team has been given $50 million of venture capital to start a company called 'Newco'. This means that they are now free to do what is right for their new business, unhindered by the restrictions of policy and politics in the old company. This also forces people to take on fresh roles focused more on the visioning work and less on their current job and can liberate a great deal of pent-up energy. People stop towing the company line and start thinking, 'What would I really do if this was my business?' Getting into a Newco frame of mind can be helped along by allocating strategic thrusts to team members rather than the central team owning all of these. Someone can be in charge of analysing the competition, another person made responsible for bringing to life the brand world and so on.

Purpose: Tombstone writing

Working on the core purpose is one of the hardest parts of the visioning process and is almost a philosophical debate. Why do we as a business exist? And would anybody care if we disappeared off the face of the earth? Along the lines of this last question is an exercise called Tombstone, where you write a brand obituary and imagine what the mourners would say at the funeral. What would people miss most? You have to work hard to get up from the functional, rational level and add an emotional dimension related to the impact that you want the brand to have on everyday life. The Body Shop in its heyday was genuinely driven by a purpose to do with raising awareness of and interest in environmental issues. This purpose influenced everything from sourcing of ingredients, through policy on animal testing to the type of packaging used.

Another exercise to try out is to take some companies who have or had a strong purpose and then imagine that the CEO (e.g. Branson, Roddick, Ben or Jerry of ice cream fame) is now running your business. The results are always skewed in the direction of the CEO's hobby-horse issues and are never useable in their entirety, but you may obtain a couple of interesting ideas.

Destination: Front page news

To work on the destination a good exercise is to have the team write a newspaper headline and front-page story from some point in the future, say 5–10 years out. What would the brand have achieved by this time that would be newsworthy? How big would the brand be and what sort of products and services is it offering? And what has happened to the competition during this time?

The hardest task when setting the destination with a team is often to challenge people to be ambitious enough. They often find it hard to get out of the mindset of thinking about how easy it will be to deliver the targets you are discussing and still get their bonus. To be clear, though, the destination you are setting is not something to be taken and put straight into the three-year plan! It is more of a stretch goal used to stimulate the team and not a profit-forecasting exercise. This is why it is so important that the vision is not only about business objectives but also about the shape you want the business to be in. For example, Ben & Jerry's wanted to double the size of the business in five years but do this while protecting the integrity of the company's values.

Strategic thrusts

By capturing ideas about specific work streams during the work on purpose and destination, you will end up with a good list of projects that can then be grouped into strategic thrusts. There do tend to be some thrusts that come back again and again and it may help you to consider the following headings as stimuli or to check that you haven't missed any key points:

- *Brand universe*: bringing to life the desired imagery, personality and benefits of the brand to help in briefing people internally and externally.
- *Consumer connection*: understanding in depth the target consumer's life, needs and attitudes.
- *Innovation*: developing new products and services to help deliver the brand vision.
- *Supply chain*: working to create efficiencies in the supply chain in order to drive down the cost of goods.
- *Organization*: working on the culture, structure and rewards to help create the right organization to deliver the vision.

The Top Clean story

The power of vision to inspire and guide a business is well illustrated by the journey that the 'Top Clean' team at Unilever has made in the four years its members have been working together. They have made huge steps towards transforming a collection of divergent laundry detergent brands into a true global brand delivering over $2 billion of sales.

David Arkwright started work as the Top Clean Global Brand Director in 1997, with the task of creating and implementing a common, global vision. This was a monumental challenge given the patchwork of different brands that he inherited, with a confusing array of positionings, pack designs and advertising. To make matters worse the brand name itself was not even the same, hence the use of the desired positioning to christen the team. In most cases the name Omo was used (Latin America, Africa, Middle East) but in others a different name existed, such as Breeze in some Asian markets. What brought these disparate bits of business together was the potential to occupy a mainstream, market-leading position focused on top cleaning performance. What had the potential to keep them apart was a group of regional brand directors who were attached to their own local position and heritage and lacked a common goal.

The first step was to convince the team of the need to change and persuade them to join the journey towards a global brand. This in itself was no mean feat, given that David had no direct authority over the regions and hardly any budget, yet needed to give clear leadership.

> I acted as if I was in the driving seat, even if I had no direct power over the people in the team; they could have easily just gone on doing business as usual. I made much of the way Unilever was moving towards global brands, using the map of the Top Clean world with its multitude of different packs to create a 'burning platform'. This helped convince people to change themselves before change was forced on them from above.

The ambition was clear and the *destination* had a deadline: to have a global brand mix in place within three to four years capable of creating double-digit growth. This had the potential to create economies of scale in packaging, production and raw materials. However, it also started to create a sense of professional pride in working on a global brand that had status and importance within the organization.

To help prove that reaching the destination was ambitious but not impossible, global research was commissioned to understand consumers in more depth. This started with qualitative work that used 'laddering' to uncover the 'higher-order' emotional benefits that consumers got from cleaning their clothes. This work showed that, among others, a seemingly big emotional benefit was having the freedom to let children play and get dirty, confident that Omo would get the toughest stains out first time. Significantly, this need was important from Bombay to Brazil. An extensive quantitative study in 22 markets served to validate the shared needs and highlight the opportunity for a common brand platform.

This consumer learning also served as a springboard for working on the brand's *purpose*. Team members challenged themselves to think about the cause they wanted to defend, the issue for which they were ready to fight. This led to the idea of 'helping parents help their kids learn and develop by getting dirty'. This brand purpose played a key role in motivating and guiding the brand team. First, it provided a new battle to fight that was bigger and more exciting than the one to defend a regional brand's historical positioning. The team had a new cause to defend that its members could rally around. Secondly, it opened up an opportunity to develop a brand mix that was truly differentiated versus the arch rival, P&G's Ariel.

A brand positioning was developed to translate the purpose into a closely linked consumer promise. This was centred on the idea of Omo having the cleaning performance needed to give parents the confidence to let their children get dirty. An advertising idea called 'No stains, no learning' brought this promise to life. It showed the emotional payoff for parents who let their kids get dirty, in contrast to years of previous advertising that had women talking artificially to camera about stains. The campaign started in Brazil during 2000 and then spread to Asia and Africa on the back of excellent testing and in-market results. In addition, the brand promise inspired a range of brand activation activity covering sponsorship and PR, such as the Turkish team which set up an Omo club to provide mums with advice on parenting and other issues, now with more than 100 000 members.

The final pieces of the visioning exercise were developing values that would serve as guiding principles and agreeing a small number of strategic thrusts. The *values* worked along the same lines as the 'liberalist' purpose, covering areas such as 'learning by doing' and 'the right to play'. Importantly, team members committed to make these values come to life by applying them to the way they worked together. For example, future ideas for new products were mocked up as prototypes rather than being summarized as conventional written concepts. The *thrusts* pinned down the actions needed to progress along the journey towards the destination of being a true global brand. For example, one of the key thrusts addressed the need to align core elements of the brand to create a more harmonized brand. This would help realize cost savings, but, more significantly, would focus the team's resources and energy on developing one breakthrough mix that was better than anything currently on the market.

The end of 2000 saw the first step towards harmonized packaging, with a common 'starburst' design idea being introduced (Figure 5.3). In addition, the vision also inspired marketing activities in key markets like Brazil, with activities such as a painting competition for children with the winning painting being featured in a poster advertising

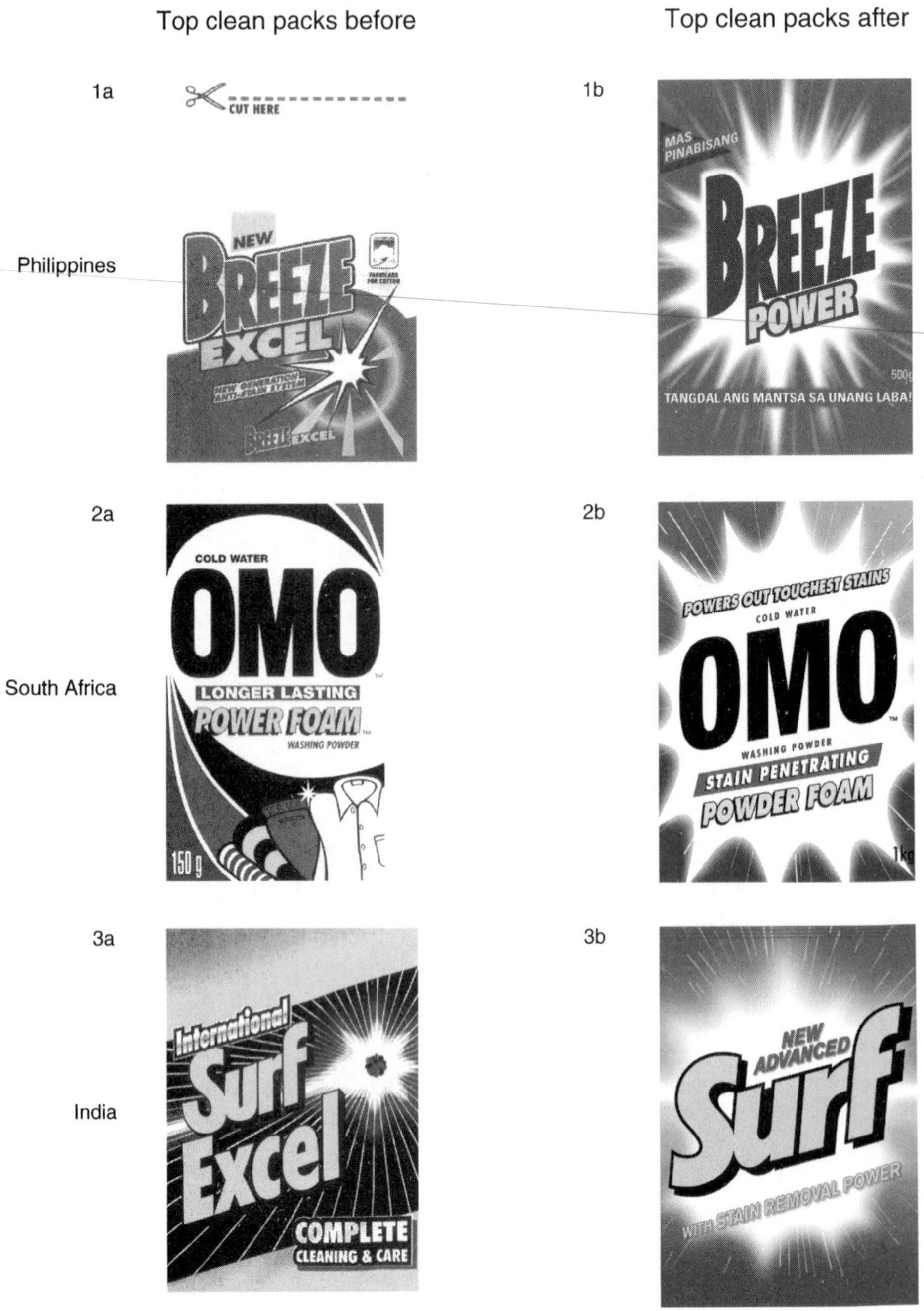

Top clean packs before

Top clean packs after

1a

1b

Philippines

2a

2b

South Africa

3a

3b

India

Figure 5.3: Top Clean packaging harmonization.

Reproduced by permission of Unilever plc.

Figure 5.4: Example of Top Clean brand activity on Omo Brazil.

Reproduced by permission of Unilever Brazil.

campaign (Figure 5.4). Early share results are positive in the regions that are working to the vision, which now include Asia, Africa and the Middle East.

If David had started with the fragmented pieces of the puzzle and tried to fit them together, he thinks that he would probably still be struggling to create a coherent picture. However, by being ambitious enough to create an alternative vision of what the brand *could* be in the future and working back to reality, he was able to mobilize the business and create the beginnings of a truly global brand.

Key takeouts

1 Vision involves being ambitious about where you want to go and how you want to get there. It should stimulate, challenge and stretch you to change the way you do business.

2 The keys to bringing a vision to life are having the right people working to a tight deadline. Be wary of processes that involve too many people and take more than a few months to complete.

3 Avoid generic mission and vision statements promising to meet the needs of shareholders, customers and employees. Be more specific and differentiated.

 ## 3-part action plan

Tomorrow

The best place to start is to understand how clear the vision is for your brand now. Talk to the people in your direct team and consult a few key stakeholders, for example in a couple of important markets or regions. Do they have a clear idea of where you are heading with the brand and what success will look and feel like? Do they connect with a purpose for the brand that goes beyond merely volume and profit growth to something a little richer in emotion and meaning? And is there a shared understanding of the five to six most important programmes that are driving the brand towards its destination?

This month

If you decide to undertake a visioning project, think carefully about the right people to form the board of directors for your 'Newco'. The level of influence on the business, often related to the size of business they run, is clearly a factor, but you also need to find people with the right attitude. Look for those with a strong point of view, who are concerned with doing the right thing to grow the business even if this ruffles a few corporate feathers. Search for team members who are not afraid by ideas of stretch, challenge and ambition. These people will also tend to be vociferous about their opinions, so if you get them on board they will be highly effective at helping you bring the vision to life.

This year

Twelve months is about the right timeframe to develop *and* start to implement a vision for your brand. By the end of the year you should see a marked difference in the way the team is working. If you have been successful in developing and bringing to life a vision for the brand, people should be more aligned and energized than before. Having a clear set of strategic thrusts makes it much easier to check on progress and ensure that resources are being put into the priority projects. Some of the thrusts themselves should also be starting to come to life and hopefully having a positive impact. Nothing succeeds like success, and if positive results are starting to appear then the next Workout, 'Keep the brand on track', will be much easier.

 ## Handover

This Workout has shown the importance of having an ambition for your brand in terms of its purpose and the destination you want to reach eventually. However, no team, no matter how great, will be able to progress easily to the desired end point in a straight line. Set-backs and diversions are inevitable in any business venture. The key is to have a way of knowing when the brand is starting to stray off course and being able then to correct the deviation and get the team moving back on the right track. The next Workout, 'Keep the brand on track', will review the role of brand positioning as a tool to help you ensure that all the team's marketing efforts are working towards your desired goals.

Workout Five: Keep the brand on track

CHAPTER 6

'Good ideas are not adopted automatically. They must be driven into practice with courageous impatience.'

Admiral Hyman G. Rickover

 Headlines

Brand positioning plays a vital role in keeping a brand on track towards its destination. It pinpoints what makes the brand motivating, different and true for target consumers. In doing so it should inspire and guide the team to help them develop a competitive and coherent brand mix. However, positioning can become a perfect example of brand bureaucracy if there is an emphasis on box filling and 'pyramid polishing'. The focus should always be kept on action and how the strategy will help build the brand and the business.

Turn on the television, read a magazine or listen to the radio and you are sure to encounter 'brand static': advertising that shouts at the top of its voice without having anything interesting to say. You have to work hard to understand where the brand is trying to go and even when you figure this out the answer often fails to motivate you. Over the years these brands veer from one creative idea to another, in a desperate and fruitless search for growth. In many cases the explanation for this lack of clarity and relevance is not a shortage of talent in the creative department, nor the absence of a motivated brand team. The answer often comes down to the team not having defined a clear positioning to help get the brand on track and keep it there.

Winning teams recognize that you can't travel to your desired destination in a straight line, in the same way that when sailing a boat you need to tack forward. They appreciate the need for something like a GPS (Global Positioning System) for brands, which tells you whether you are on track and suggests when you need to change direction (Figure 6.1). This

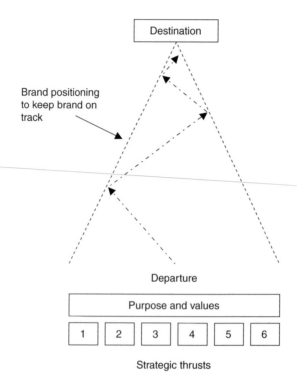

Figure 6.1: Brand positioning to help navigation.

ensures that over time a 'brand story' starts to build, with changes in execution used for refreshment and rejuvenation and not to change the positioning itself. Look at a reel of advertising for a brand such as Volvo and you will see a good example of a brand story. There is a consistent focus on safety, but the expressions of this message become more aspirational and contemporary, underpinned by new cars like the S40 that are solid yet more attractive.

The need for a brand positioning that helps keep the team on track is becoming more important as the number of people involved in developing and delivering the brand mix becomes bigger. More and more agencies are involved, covering PR, events, online and guerrilla marketing. And many brands are now being run globally, with the need to align and engage regions and markets to head in the same direction. The positioning should help *inspire* people in the team to develop great marketing. Consider everything BMW does, from its website to the cars and the showrooms, and you will see a clear positioning. Each element communicates the core values of 'performance', 'technology', 'exclusivity' and 'quality', with a consistent tone and style based on black, silver and grey. Advertising agency WCRS not only developed the Ultimate Driving Machine advertising campaign, it had a leading role in communicating the brand values internally to the dealer network. The importance of these efforts in building the brand was shown by the starring role played by agency chairman Robin Wight in the training videos. The results for BMW are clear, with sales growing from 13 000 in 1979 to over 75 000 today and the number of dealers staying roughly the same.

At the same time the positioning should *guide* team members by telling them whether activities or actions are on or off strategy and helping in the selection of the right ones. If the Disney's positioning is about childhood fun, magic and entertainment, then promotional partners should ideally share the same values. Breakfast cereals are an ideal link-up as they are enjoyable, interactive and wholesome. Toilet rolls and petrol are less obvious opportunities.

In this Workout we will look at the building blocks of brand positioning and how to use them to inspire and guide you in the development of a business-building brand mix.

Content is king

Like all strategy, positioning is the process of answering a few simple but important questions, such as 'Who is your core consumer?' and 'Why should they buy your brand?' Above all, positioning is about sacrifice and avoiding the 'air raid shelter' syndrome that so often trips teams up. Here, people put every idea possible into the positioning and so end up with a strategy that is flabby, unfocused and not much use to anyone. This problem is aggravated when a committee writes the positioning, as this always leads to a watered-down compromise without any edge.

In contrast, when it is clearly and tightly defined, positioning can be a central tool for helping boost return on brand investment. It inspires and guides the team, giving a clear picture of both the 'job' the brand needs to do and the 'human side' to be reflected in tone and feel. It should become an integral part of how the brand is run and not be a piece of paper that gathers dust in the cupboard.

When working on positioning, never forget that content is king: the way you present the output is of absolutely no importance whatsoever. No matter how hard a consultancy tries to sell you its latest onion, doughnut or flying saucer-shaped tool, don't believe its staff when they say that theirs is better. *They are all the same.* They might look different, but the fundamental questions are identical. What *is* important is that within a company everyone uses the *same* tool, definitions and format. Speaking the same language is crucial to facilitate effective communication. However, the choice of the language itself is irrelevant as long as everyone is fluent in it.

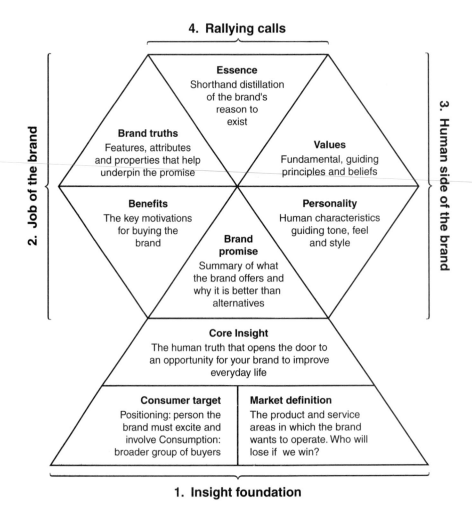

Figure 6.2: Example positioning tool (pick your own shape).

The questions that need to be addressed by any positioning tool fall into four main categories and are summarized in Figure 6.2. (Feel free to pick your own shape if you don't like the one proposed.) The four areas that the tool covers are insight foundation, job of the brand, human side of the brand and rallying calls.

Ben & Jerry's ice-cream cone

The different elements of a positioning should come together as a coherent whole with a 'red thread' that links them together. In most strong brands this thread starts with one or more brand truths, providing real substance and content that can be the starting point for a compelling and unique 'story'. In contrast, weak brands have a hollow core devoid of any truth, and the positioning exercise is about inventing points of difference when none really exists.

One of the best examples of a brand with real truth behind it is Ben & Jerry's, who have a series of policies and ways of working that underpin their social mission. They donate 10 per cent of all profits to charity and purchase raw materials from groups they want to support, such as milk from the endangered Vermont farmers. Brands like this are a pleasure to do strategic work on, as they have a true story to tell and the task is to find the most interesting angle on which to position the brand.

For many years Ben & Jerry's was a brand led by its founders and focused on the US market, with little need for a clearly defined brand-positioning strategy. However, when the company was bought by Unilever for $326 million, there was a need to capture a positioning enabling the brand idea to be communicated to a much wider internal audience. International expansion leveraging Unilever's global distribution network was one of the key ways of adding value to Ben & Jerry's, but the teams of people working on this development needed briefing on the brand.

In typical fashion, the team chose not to employ the standard Unilever format but instead used an ice-cream cone. A positioning for the brand is illustrated in Figure 6.3, with its heart being the genuineness of the ingredients and the mission of the company, delivering 'joy for the belly *and* soul', as CEO Yves Couette describes the brand's essence (1). This is all wrapped up with a quirky, irreverent personality, visible in flavours such as Funky Monkey.

 ## 5-minute workout

Take out the positioning tool that you have for one of your key brands. Whatever the format, does it answer the key questions described so far? Use the tips and tricks to do a quick review and spot areas that need work. Also, see if there is a red thread that ties the elements of the positioning together in the same way as with Ben & Jerry's.

The building blocks of positioning

We will now look in more detail at the building blocks of brand positioning and how they work to inspire and guide the development of a competitive and coherent brand mix. The

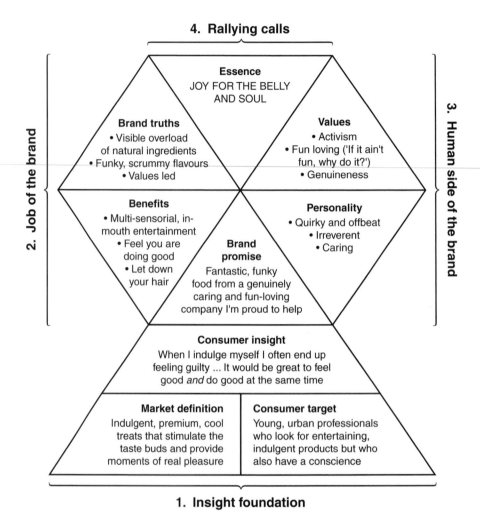

Figure 6.3: Ben & Jerry's positioning tool (author's own).

practical use of each element and some tips and tricks on developing them are given in Table 6.1. You may want to review this list and decide which of the positioning elements you want to focus on over the next few pages.

Insight foundation

Most great brands are built on a strong foundation of insight. Get this part right and you are well on the way to developing a competitive and coherent positioning. Get it wrong

Table 6.1: Positioning tips and tricks

Group		Inspires and guides	Tips and tricks	Bad examples	Good examples
Insight foundation	**Market definition**	Full view of real competition Ideas for stretch	Who wins when we lose? Use benefits not just product terms	Videotapes (Blockbuster)	Rentable home entertainment (Blockbuster)
	Positioning target	Empathy with the core consumer, understand their life	Capture attitudes, values, colour	AB women aged 25–45 (Knorr)	Food enthusiasts who enjoy good food but are pressed for time (Knorr)
	Core insight	Open the door to an opportunity to improve everyday life	Describe a human truth *and* how this opens a door for the brand Add colour and emotion	Parents worry about nappy rash (Pampers)	People who are concerned about their baby having a wet bottom and getting nappy rash as this makes them worry about not being a perfect parent (Pampers)
Job of brand	**Brand truths (limit to 2–3)**	Development of product features and attributes	Be specific and concrete	Good service (Blockbuster)	Blockbuster promise: 'Get the film you want or hire it for free next time'
	Benefits (limit to 2–3)	Product development, communication emphasis	Specific reasons for purchase, not reasons to believe	Pro-vitamin B5; doesn't dry hair (Pantene)	'Hair so healthy it shines' (Pantene)
Human side	**Values (limit to 2–3)**	Issues to campaign on, brand behaviours with customers	Make them provocative and polarizing	Quality, teamwork (Prêt à Manger)	Setting the bar high, one for all, all for one (Prêt à Manger)
	Personality (limit to 3–4)	Guide tone, feel and style of communication and front-line staff	Make them colourful not bland	Reliable, honest, friendly (Clearasil)	Solid as a rock, straight as an arrow, best mate (Clearasil)
Rallying calls	**Promise (limit to 15–20 words)**	Key summary input for briefs	Focused on what it is and why it is better Inject colour, emotion and edge	Affordable short-break holiday offering best combination of activities for all the family (DLP)	Magical place where everyone can live out adventures they have dreamt of (DLP)
	Essence (limit to 2–4 words)	Shorthand check for reviewing the brand mix	Capture emotion not just function, inspire future growth	Best shave (Gillette), male attractiveness (Lynx)	Ultimate performance (Gillette), Pulling power (Lynx)

and you will struggle. We will look at three specific areas of insight: market definition, positioning target and core insight.

Market definition

The market definition should keep the team in touch with who the brand is competing with, both directly and indirectly. 'Who wins when we lose?' is the key question to ask. A common mistake is to use manufacturer terms, such as 'olive oil', 'shampoo' or 'mobile phone'. This gives a narrow view of the world and breeds a false sense of security, as Levi's found to its cost in the 1990s. The company saw itself as competing in the 'jeans' market and focused on building share here. However, young people saw jeans as just one possible alternative in their wardrobe of casual clothing and when cargo pants and combat trousers came on the scene they started buying those instead. Levi's was really in the 'casual apparel' market, a better and broader definition of the choices that consumers had. The *direct* competitors were other jeans brands like Lee and Wrangler, but the *real* competitors were casual fashion labels like Zara and more upmarket brands like Emporio Armani.

A broader market definition is also a good stimulus for innovation, as it opens your eyes to new needs that the brand could meet. This is becoming more important as companies focus on fewer brands that need to stretch and offer a much bigger range. Lynx started with a narrow, product-based market definition of *'Deodorant and anti-perspirant body sprays'*. However, to provide the platform for a much bigger, multi-product brand, a better definition is: *'Products and services which help young men feel more self-confident and attractive.'* Lynx is now selling shampoo and shower gel to compete in this broader market.

You can of course go too broad in the definition and end up so wide that it will not give any guidance on appropriate product innovation. Getting the right balance comes down to your judgement and some idea of how ambitious you want to be in stretching the brand. The brand's purpose from the Workout on 'Bring your vision to life' can be a useful input to getting the right market definition. For example, there would be a direct link between Blockbuster's purpose of 'Making a night in as entertaining as a night out' and a market definition of 'rentable home entertainment'.

Positioning target

Having a vivid and colourful picture of the positioning target is essential to help team members develop a brand mix that really meets their needs, as people not just as product users. It is an area of positioning that often receives little attention, yet it is a vital step in the process. You cannot get a rich and deep insight with a two-dimensional view of the core target. A tightly defined profile should be based on attitudes, values and needs, not merely sociodemographics such as 'men 18–35' (Figure 6.4). It defines the sort of person the brand mix will be designed for. A broader set of people, the consumption target, will end up buying the product (Figure 6.5). They may aspire to the same values but not practice them all the time. A conservative office worker might drink wine during the week but on Friday night be closer to the 'wild child' who could be the positioning target for Bacardi Breezer.

Taking Levi's again, the brand's positioning target is fashion-conscious, active, urban people aged in their late teens and early twenties. When these people wear the brand and

Attitudes to life Guiding principles which influence approach to life in general (e.g. ambitious, live life for today, concern for environment)	**Interest centres** What they like to spend their time and money on (e.g. exotic holidays, gadgets, sport)
Needs Functional and emotional needs from the category (e.g. refreshment, status, indulgence)	**Sociodemographics** Centre of gravity of group in terms of age, sex, social class etc.

Figure 6.4: Positioning target.

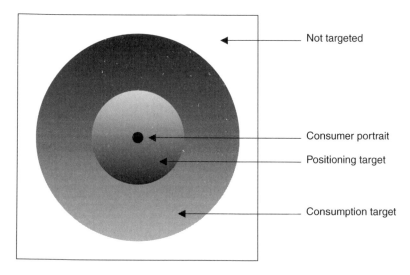

Figure 6.5: Consumer targets.

think it is cool then more mainstream, older people will follow suit. However, in the mid-1990s the brand's marketing was really only appealing to older, less fashionable people and the younger target started to switch off. The mix had lost the edge needed to appeal to a younger audience. When the company focused on winning back the youth market with twisted jeans and a more radical form of advertising, the brand returned to growth.

Brand teams often shy away from having a tight target definition, as they fear losing users and want *everyone* to buy their brand. However, a narrowly defined positioning target is more likely to inspire and guide the creation of a compelling and motivating brand mix that will appeal to a wide range of people. In contrast, try to appeal to a broader target and you may end up with a safe and boring mix that excites no one. Often creative teams find that the most helpful way of presenting a positioning target is to paint a 'consumer portrait' of an individual, as was done for the Russian beer Golden Barrel that we saw in an earlier Workout. The imaginary guy we were after was christened Sergei and one of the key attitudes the portrait brought to life was 'solidarity':

> Sergei's friends are important to him and he always tries to stand by them. When times were tough and one friend lost his job at the factory, Sergei put him forward for a job in the market where he worked.

Core insight

The core insight is a human truth that opens the door to an opportunity for your brand to improve the everyday lives of its consumers. Get the insight right and you are half way to cracking the whole brand positioning, as it will inspire and guide the other elements. Watch out here for getting only as far as a 'finding', an observation of consumer behaviour or attitudes that is factually true but superficial and rational in nature. The core insight needs to go deeper and tap into the emotions that people feel, not merely the things they do and say. For Pampers, we could summarize the core insight as:

> Parents are concerned about their baby having a wet bottom and getting nappy rash … and this makes them worried about not being a perfect mum or dad.

The concern about nappy rash is a human truth to which any parent can relate. However, the challenge is to open the door presented by this truth and uncover the opportunity for the brand by tapping into the consumer at a deeper, more emotional level. In this case, it is the concern about making a mistake for that little person who can't tell you what you are doing wrong that is the real issue. Pampers responds to this opportunity with a promise

Table 6.2: Insight generators

Market definition

1 If your product or service was suddenly no longer available, what other product would people use in place of it?
2 When you win consumers, who loses?
3 Draw a series of concentric circles with each one a little bigger than the last. In the middle write the products that are closest to what your brand offers now (shampoo, for example), then in the next circle ones that are related but a bit further away (conditioners) and so on. When you have filled in five or six circles, find a way of describing the entire contents of all the circles.

Core insight

1 When are the results of product failure or success most important, and how do people feel when this happens?
2 What is the improvement, however small, that using the product brings into everyday life?
3 What would people miss the most if the product disappeared for ever?
4 If the name of the brand that someone was using in the category was visible, such as being written on a t-shirt, what would it say about them and how would it make them feel?
5 The 'toddler test': ask people why they use your product category and when you get an answer keep asking 'Why?' until you get to a deeper, more emotional level of understanding.

---

offering mums and dads 'reassurance and support so they can feel confident of being the best parent possible'. The brand has taken a fairly serious and considered approach to parenting, compared to Huggies' more light-hearted and entertaining approach. Advertising has featured 'expert mothers', such as nursery supervisors, who rely on the brand. The brand is sampled in hospitals so that new mums use Pampers as the first nappy on their baby, creating a strong emotional bond. The brand has recently tapped further into the idea of babies being little people who can't communicate verbally through its campaign 'Learning from babies', which helps you understand how they see the world. All these activities feed off the insight that parents, especially new mums and dads, want to do everything possible to be good at their new role in life.

A series of 'insight generators' to help in developing the core insight and market definition are summarized in Table 6.2.

Job of the brand

Most great brands have at their heart a great product or service that does an important job for consumers. They deliver a customer experience that lives up to or exceeds the image portrayed in communication. This requires the definition of brand truths and brand benefits that flow from these.

Brand truths

Brand truths are the seeds from which relevant and motivating benefits can be grown. People are interested in the story behind a brand and are prepared to pay a little more when there are some authentic, genuine credentials. A list of different types of brand truth is shown in Table 6.3. A truth can be something physical, such as the pro-vitamin B5 active ingredient in Pantene shampoo or Andrex's 'softer, longer and stronger' toilet tissue. The truth can also be more intangible, such as the American roots of Levi's and the use of Ray Ban sunglasses by the US air force.

Brand truths need to be as specific as possible and avoid throwaway words such as 'quality', 'service' and 'convenience'. A brilliant example of a concrete brand truth is the 'Blockbuster Promise' guaranteeing that you can get the film of your choice or rent it for free next time. The promise is made possible because the company is able to stock a huge number of copies of each major film through a unique revenue-sharing scheme with the film studios. Blockbuster pays only a fraction of the normal price up front for the tapes or DVDs, thus limiting capital expenditure, but then pays the studios a share of the revenue. Everyone is a winner: consumers get the film they want, Blockbuster rents more films through the increased traffic generated by the promise and the studios end up gaining more revenue.

Brand benefits

Brand truths in themselves are of course useless unless they translate into concrete and motivating reasons to buy the brand. Indeed, product features are often mistaken for benefits. A way to check that you are on the right track is to be sure that you are talking about

Table 6.3: Searching for brand truths

Truth	Probe	Example
1 History	When was the brand created, where and by whom?	Levi's
2 Ingredients	What are they, how do they work and what are they called?	Pantene
3 Form	What are the distinguishing characteristics, such as colour, texture, thickness etc.?	Guinness
4 Users	Are there any current or past users who can add credibility and relevance?	Ray-Ban
5 Manufacturing	Are there any unique aspects of how the product is made that can help tell a story?	Prêt à Manger
6 People	What distinguishing features do front-line staff have that make the service different?	Egg
7 Values	Is there a brand 'cause' that the company fights for and takes a stand on?	Ben & Jerry's
8 Consistency	Do you deliver a more consistent and reliable service?	Amazon

something that is genuinely a motivation for buying the brand. In the case of Blockbuster the benefit flowing from its promise is 'being confident I'll get the film I want'. The strongest brands tend to have benefits that are a mix of both the functional (e.g. gets rid of dandruff from the first wash) and emotional (e.g. gives me confidence when it counts most).

Human side of the brand

You could argue that if a brand does its basic job well it has no need for a human dimension. However, values and personality can add significant value, helping turn a good product into a great brand. First, they allow the brand to develop a much more powerful connection with the people who buy and use it, tapping into the purchasers' own values and personality. To use the analogy of a doctor, you might see one for the first time and find that he does a competent job of diagnosing your problem and correctly prescribing a course of treatment. However, if he is aggressive, scruffily dressed and is a blatant sexist, you may decide not to see him again. The reason for your choice is less to do with functional benefits and more to do with the doctor's values and personality. In the same way, you build relationships with those brands that deliver against the rational needs you have but also have an extra dimension that works at a more emotional level.

Claiming that a shampoo or washing powder can have a personality may seem far-fetched, but a simple projective exercise shows that it is true. Ask someone in the UK to imagine the sort of people the Ariel and Persil brands of washing powder would be if they came to life and you will get very different responses. Persil is a caring mum who looks after her kids and wants them to look their best, whereas Ariel is a male scientist dedicated to finding the best solution to your problems (2).

Values
Values are the fundamental beliefs and principles of the brand. They should guide the battles that the brand wants to fight and the issues that it seeks to defend. For a real person having a clear set of values helps you make important decisions and navigate through life. If 'leadership' is an important value for someone they may seek to play an active role in guiding the direction of the teams in which they work, whereas someone who believes strongly in 'environmental protection' may seek out biodegradable packaging and prefer public transport to the car. Strong brands also need to have clear values, especially corporate brands like Virgin, Tesco and Body Shop where the brand people buy and the company that sells it are the same. Here, the leaders and their actions are highly visible to

consumers. In the case of Tesco, the brand has actively campaigned for the right to sell fashion brands such as Levi's at knockdown prices by importing cheap products from outside the UK. In this way Tesco is demonstrating a value of 'consumer rights', portraying itself as a defender of access to the best product at the lowest price. However, values can also guide the actions of product brands, as we saw in the Top Clean story when the brand promoted the idea of letting children play and get dirty.

There should be a linkage between the brand values and those from the company vision that we saw in the Workout 'Bring your vision to life'. However, this is likely to be crossover but not duplication. Taking the example of Gillette and its shavers, among the company's values of 'integrity', 'collaboration' and 'achievement' only the latter is probably of relevance in consumer positioning. This in turn may have additional values such as 'performance' and 'confidence'.

Personality

Personality is the set of human characteristics that guide the tone, feel and style of the brand. It is less profound in nature than the brand values, although it is nonetheless important in transforming a product into a brand. Indeed, tone, feel and style can be a key source of differentiation between brands. On the Cointreau brand the product itself had many inherent strengths: enjoyable orange taste, alcoholic kick, true spirit credentials and authentic roots. However, as we saw earlier in the Workout on 'Searching for true insight', the brand was held back by a dusty and old-fashioned image. A new and more appealing personality emerged from the brand truth about how the warm orangeness of the product contrasted with the coolness of the ice. This new personality had statements such as 'sensual', 'elegance with attitude' and 'smoulderingly stylish'. This inspired a revamped bottle design that helped increase shelf impact and gain distribution in the crucial US market (Figure 6.6). It is also reflected in press advertising that portrays a new face of Cointreau (Figure 6.7). After 15 years of continuous decline and a halving of brand volumes, the brand increased sales by 10 per cent in the five years following the re-launch. This stronger brand performance was also a key factor in doubling the share price of parent company Rémy Cointreau.

One trap to avoid when creating an emotional connection is showing a mirror up to the consumer by simply playing back their own values and personality. In some cases this can work, but most of the time people have a different sort of relationship in mind (Table 6.4). For example, the Clearasil range of acne products had a personality described as 'Your best mate who you can rely on. The brand needs to act and behave like a best friend, with whom you would share your hopes and fears and be confident that they would support and help you.

Before: classic, dusty, old-fashioned

After: sensual, stylish, elegant

Figure 6.6: Impact of brand personality on Cointreau bottle.

Reproduced by permission of Rémy Cointreau.

Rallying calls

A positioning needs to capture quite a lot of detail about a brand covering insight foundations, the job of the brand and the human side. It is a detailed summary of what makes the brand different and relevant to its target market. However, it is impossible for people to

Table 6.4: Brand–consumer relationships

Relationship	Brand role	Example	
Ally	Support and encourage	Clearasil	Inner directed
Advice	Reassure and give confidence	NatWest	↑
Like you	Understand and help	Persil	
Aspiration	Inspire, excite and offer status	Nike	
Rebellion	Thrill and excite	Diesel	↓
Cause	Make a statement	Ben & Jerry's	Outer directed

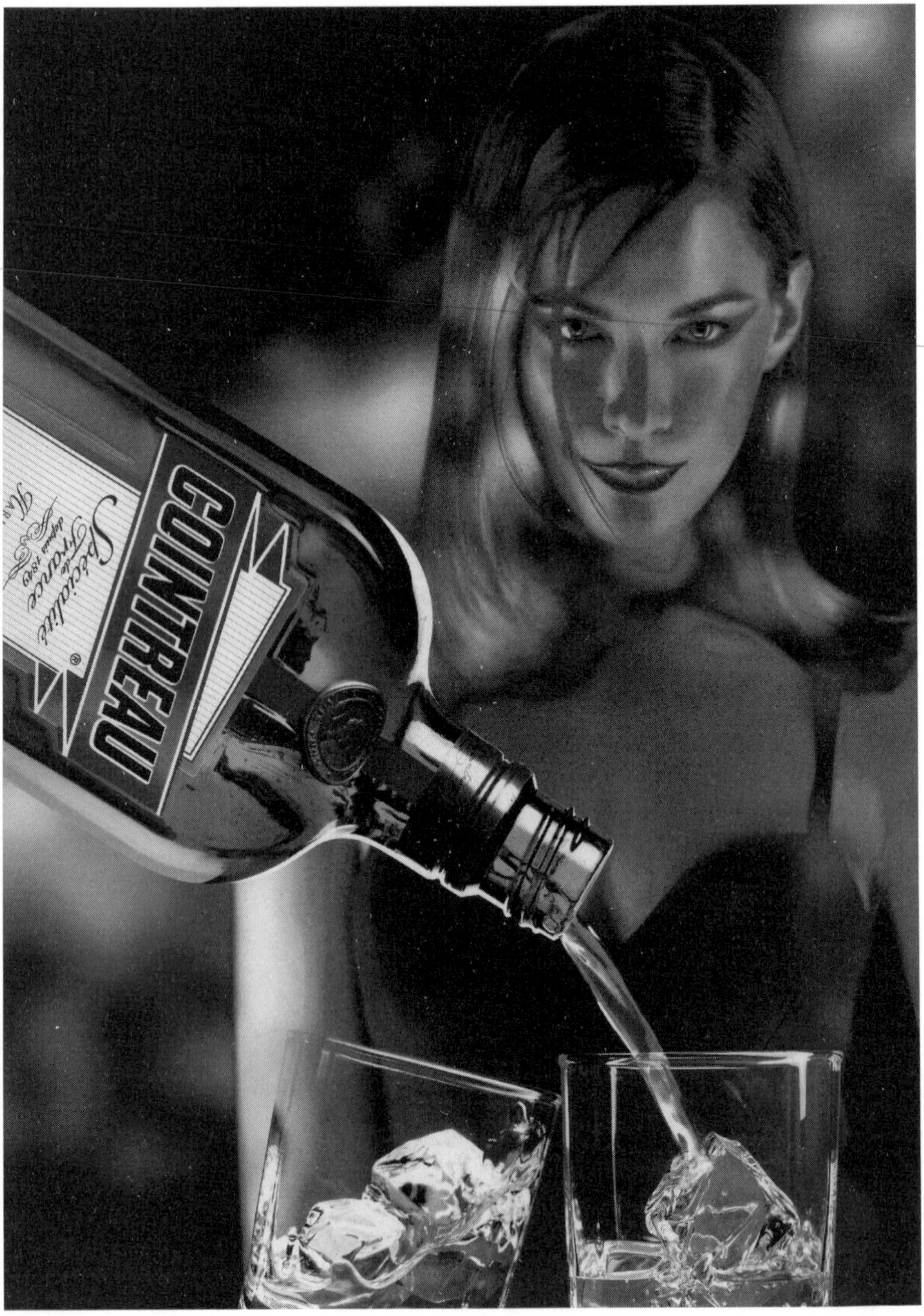

Figure 6.7: The new image of Cointreau.

Reproduced by permission of Rémy Cointreau.

keep all the content of the strategy in their heads, especially as they are likely to work on more than one brand. Therefore, it can be very helpful to have some 'rallying calls' that serve as shorthand reminders of the brand positioning.

Brand promise

The brand promise summarizes the customer experience being offered. Drawing on the positioning as a whole, it should emphasize the key aspects that create relevance and differentiation and so drive preference. Defining and delivering against a clear promise is of course what brands are all about. Your weekly supermarket trip takes one hour not one day as you zip past most fixtures, picking brands that you know and trust quickly and easily. The brand promise is best kept to no more than 20 words, and should summarize 'what' the brand offers and 'why' it is better than alternatives. The challenge is to strip out as many words as possible to get to the sharpest, shortest phrase; teams often find this hard because they are afraid of missing stuff out.

Differentiation is usually anchored in a benefit, but may also be centred on another segmentation variable such as the occasion, price or target. In the case of the re-launch 07 107of EuroDisney, the promise was:

> A magical land (what) where people of all ages (who) can live out the adventures they have dreamt of (why).

Brand essence

Brand essence is a shorthand distillation of the brand's reason to exist. It is one of the hardest and least well-understood parts of brand positioning and can use up weeks of valuable time without helping improve mix effectiveness. The risk is merely doing a retrospective exercise of finding one or two words that summarize what made the brand unique among its peers in the past. For example, you could theorize that Nike is all about 'winning' or 'success' or that BMW is the brand of 'ambition'. This can work for a strong brand that stands for something you want to protect, where the focus is *keeping* the brand on track. However, when a brand is weak or new there is little or nothing of the past to distil down. Here, a more action-oriented and future-focused approach is required. A shorthand phrase is needed to capture what you *want* the brand ultimately to stand for, in a way that inspires and guides the team's efforts. If you can get this down to four, three or even two words then you have a chance of people actually remembering it. A way to think about this is to consider it as something you would want to write on the brand t-shirt or baseball cap at a brand conference.

For example, on the Pilsner Urquell brand of beer the team found a series of truths linked to the fact that it was the first ever pilsner, clear and crisp where all products before were cloudy. However, being 'the original pilsner' by itself lacked the emotional pull to work as a rallying call. Research with consumers and people in the business showed that what was more exciting was the idea that originals, whether they are products or people, inspire you to be more original yourself. This led to the essence being defined as 'Inspiring Originality'. This essence had a direct impact on the brand mix. The pack design was revamped to better express the essence, with a striking curve added to the label (Figure 6.8). This new bottle was a key factor in helping the brand extend its distribution in the United States. In addition, an advertising idea of 'Original is better' showed how original versions were often better than later copies, such as Sean Connery being a better Bond than Roger Moore.

The concept of 'launch and learn' from the 'Get real' Workout should be kept in mind. Brand essence often evolves after the team has started to develop the marketing mix and in particular brand communication. Many brand teams try to develop an essence as memorable and impactful as an advertising slogan, agonizing over the words. A better way forward is to agree an essence that has the right *content* and move on to the creative briefing process. In many cases the creative development will provide a spark of inspiration, a bit of

Before: First pilsner on earth   After: Inspiring original

Figure 6.8: Re-launch of Pilsner Urquell reflecting new essence.

Reproduced by permission of Pilsner Urquell International.

grit in the oyster if you like, which can add the magic touch you want. Also, if you do get a slogan that is a perfect summary of the brand's reason to exist, don't slave over finding an alternative set of words for the essence, as some theoretical texts suggest you do. It might not be 'correct' to use the tag line as the essence, but if you have something as good as 'The ultimate driving machine', 'Just do it' or 'Every little bit helps', why not use it as a rallying call? This is certainly what BMW does with its brand-building efforts.

Evaluating the positioning

Any positioning should stand up against three key criteria by being motivating, different and true (Figure 6.9).

Motivating

The positioning should of course be relevant to the target consumer, meeting needs at both a functional and an emotional level. There should be a clear idea of the relationship between the brand and the consumer and this needs to be appropriate to the category in question.

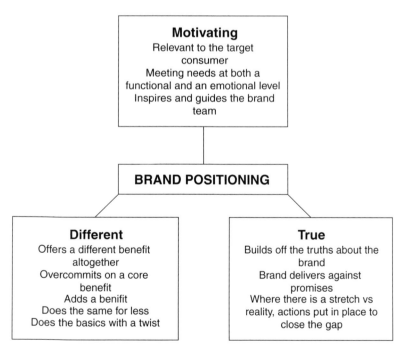

Figure 6.9: Brand positioning criteria.

Aspiration is important for a sports shoe brand, but with a bank you may be more concerned with trust and reliability. As important as turning on the consumer, if not more so, is inspiring and guiding the brand team and creative agencies. Does the positioning give you a clear and motivating idea of where the brand should and should not go to stay on course? Are there some interesting and exciting nuggets in the positioning that get the creative juices flowing?

Different

The level of differentiation that can and should be captured in a positioning strategy is a subject for debate that we will return to in the next Workout, 'Think different *and* do different'. There is a limit to how different the strategy itself can be, as it relies on words on paper when much of differentiation is down to execution and delivery. In addition, many brands want to go for a centre-ground positioning and cannot be completely different or they risk becoming a niche player.

However, the team should push to make the positioning as differentiated as possible. It is the totality of the positioning that should be different from other brands, but the promise is the place where the brand's single most persuasive reason to choose should be summarised. Five ways of differentiating a positioning that you could consider are:

- Offer a different benefit altogether (e.g. Olivio and longevity supported by its olive oil ingredient and Mediterranean imagery).
- Re-define a core benefit (e.g. Pantene changed the definition of beautiful hair from condition and shape to 'hair so healthy it shines').
- Overcommit on a core benefit (e.g. Volvo being the safest car to protect your family).
- Add a benefit (e.g. Fairy detergent cleans well but also cares for delicate clothes).
- Do the same for less (e.g. Skoda cars now offer Volkswagen technology at a more accessible price).

True

It goes without saying that breaking your promises is bad for any relationship and brand building is no exception to the rule. A positioning needs to build on the truths about the consumer and brand to have a chance of working. If there is a big stretch between the positioning and the current reality, as may often be the case when a brand is being relaunched, there needs to be a clear action plan showing how the product or service will be upgraded to support the vision and deliver against the promise.

The Space Mountain story

Many brand issues, such as unsuccessful line extension, are symptoms of a deeper problem: the lack of a clear positioning strategy. A real-life example of this happened in 1994 when EuroDisney was struggling with the question of how to support a new multimillion-dollar attraction called Space Mountain. Much was resting on a successful launch as the park was in serious trouble. Attendances were down and well below the optimistic forecasts made on opening and the press was full of rumours of bankruptcy or even closure.

The team's dilemma was how heavily to promote the new attraction, as it was a great deal more grown up and thrilling than most of the others in the park. It featured a unique launch mechanism that employed the same technology as catapults fighter planes off air-craft carriers. The speed at the top of the launch phase, before heading down into the attraction, was actually enough to experience zero gravity and be lifted out of your seat. Once inside, you would fly through asteroid belts and loop-the-loop twice before coming into land. The whole ride was beautifully themed on the Jules Verne tale 'From the Earth to the Moon'. But should such an exciting and almost 'white knuckle' ride take the lion's share of next year's budget? Or was it better to invest behind the core park offer?

Two simple questions to help work through the issue left the Disney team somewhat perplexed: 'What is the positioning strategy of Space Mountain?' and 'How does this fit with the desired positioning of EuroDisney?' It was quickly obvious that there was no agreed positioning for the park or the new attraction. A quick look at the reel of advertis-ing used since the park's launch showed a classic case of 'brand static': the brand had tried everything from price promotion to travelogue-style fly-throughs of the park. The team agreed to work on pinning down the positioning of EuroDisney and the role of Space Mountain in helping bring this to life.

The first key finding was the importance of the planned re-launch of the park as 'Disneyland Paris' (DLP) to communicate that this was the real Disneyland, in Paris. Non-visitors saw EuroDisney as a watered-down, smaller and less impressive version of the US parks and so not the real Disney experience. However, visitors to the park confirmed the company's belief that this was not the case, with the attractions seen as some of the best in the world. Also, the smaller size of the park was not an issue as it was a destination for long weekends, much more accessible than Florida or California. Therefore a key truth for the positioning was the range of great attractions that only Disney could offer.

The second key finding was that many parents had stayed away because of concerns that EuroDisney would only be of interest to small children, leaving them as passive spectators. Again, learning from visitors showed the reality to be very different, with a good balance of safer, gentler rides plus more exciting ones. The brand promise we saw earlier for DLP was developed to pin down the active, rather than passive, nature of the experience and its appeal to everyone, whatever their age:

> Disneyland Paris is a magical land where people of all ages can live out the adventures they have dreamt of.

With a clearer idea of the core brand promise, attention could then be turned to Space Mountain. To explore the new attraction with potential visitors, mocked-up pictures were used, accompanied by a script that talked viewers through the experience. The feedback was unanimous: people loved it. It did have the excitement and thrill factor that the Disney team had anticipated, but these sensations were an integral part of an amazing, themed adventure. The adventure of going from the earth to the moon was one that everyone had dreamt of, so it was a fantastic dramatization of the total DLP positioning. What is more, the theme was even based on a French writer rather a Hollywood epic, appealing to Parisians who had turned their nose up at what they saw as an American cultural invasion on their doorstep.

It was agreed that Space Mountain would be the 'star product' in the portfolio of attractions on offer in 1994, the 'Levi's 501 of the park'. In consequence, a significant part of the annual budget was put behind the launch. This was announced with a spectacular commercial that depicted the countdown and take-off of the ship in which the visitors would 'fly'. A flash of inspiration inspired by consumer feedback was to show only the outside of the attraction and not to reveal the ride itself. Excitement and drama built as the rocket ship shot up the side of the mountain, but the film cut as it reached the top. The relaunch as Disneyland Paris, with Space Mountain in a starring role, was a huge success. Visitor numbers grew significantly and the park went into profit, going on to become the biggest tourist attraction in Europe by a long stretch.

Back to the future of your brand

Defining a competitive and compelling positioning for your brand requires you to look back as well as forward to the future. You need to search for things that have made the brand successful in the past at the same time as identifying the baggage that needs to be dropped. We looked at this earlier in the section on uncovering brand truths. However, you then need to look for ways to reinterpret the brand's strength in a way that is relevant and contemporary. This is about where you want to take your brand, the route you need to navigate to get to your desired destination, and this makes it a difficult area to research with consumers.

As we saw in the earlier Workout 'Search for true insight', research always looks through a rear-view mirror of the world. It is based on current perceptions of markets and brands and this is a particularly important limitation when working on brand positioning. It is hard for consumers to try to project themselves into the future and imagine things in a different way, especially when a brand is seeking to re-position itself or stretch into new areas behind a bigger idea. If Dove has spent many years and millions of pounds telling people that it is 'a bar for cleaning the skin without drying it out like soap', it is quite a leap to consider the brand as now selling deodorant. 'Oh, that doesn't work at all!' protests the Dove user. 'Dove is all about cleansing and caring, not about horrible smelly armpits!'

Pull the brand apart

The brand team needs to work hard to project into the future and ensure that there is enough 'stretch' in the positioning ideas that are developed. When working on a new strategy it helps to consider different possible directions in which the brand could go, and then push these as far as possible to make them different. A common mistake is to develop four to five concepts that are all fairly similar, making it hard for anyone to understand the different ideas. You are better off making the alternative directions as extreme as possible, even if this provokes a negative reaction from consumers. In this way you will get a good idea of the boundaries that the brand currently has in terms of its credibility in offering different benefits. An example of different positioning directions, in the case of a brand of rum looking to re-position, is shown in Table 6.5.

Table 6.5: Positioning directions for a rum brand

Direction	Brand truth	Key benefits	Tone and feel
1 'The real side of rum'	Favourite brand of the islanders, not just for tourists	Authenticity, in the know	Rough and real
2 'Smooth and silky'	Smooth on the way down versus other rums, even when neat	Taste enjoyment, laid back	Warm and cosy
3 'Adventure'	Long-time sponsor of sailing	Excitement, escape	Aspirational, nautical
4 'The original'	Oldest brand of rum in world	Connoisseurship, savouring	Sepia tones, olde-worlde

Bring the ideas to life

The tendency to rely on written concepts to describe new positioning ideas makes the task of trying to imagine the future even harder, as the stimulus is so poor and uninspiring. Take a written concept about a new idea that breaks some rules, present it to a bunch of eight strangers sat around a table with another group of people sat watching them, and you have all the ingredients necessary for a good game of Innokill. It happens every night of the week in a 'viewing facility' near you.

You have to be much cleverer and creative to help consumers get over the credibility gaps that your new positioning might create, suspending disbelief to give the idea a chance. Taking some of the money allocated to positioning research and re-investing this in bringing the ideas to life always pays off handsomely. It can mess around with timings a little and mean that there are fewer focus groups to go around, but it is worth it every time. Concepts can be brought to life as *brandcepts*, a combination of images to express the desired personality and words to summarize the brand promise. Increasingly, video and music are being used to be ever more effective in bringing the desired tone and feel to life. *Prototypes* of new products, packaging and services are also an effective way of visualizing a future positioning. This was the approach used to help revitalize one of the world's best-known board games: Scrabble.

The Scrabble story

When Paul McGarry started work on Scrabble in the mid-1990s, following Mattel's acquisition of the Spears company, he inherited a brand with over 50 years of proud heritage. Its positioning was summarized as 'The world's leading word game'. This captured accurately the brand's functional credentials, but fell short of inspiring and guiding the team towards the future. Sales growth on the brand was slowing down and it was agreed that the time had come to rejuvenate it. In particular, there was a need to revamp the classic, 'green baize' pack that kept Scrabble locked firmly in the past (Figure 6.10).

An initial phase of consumer exploration was a sobering experience. Scrabble was seen by the younger non-users that the brand team wanted to recruit as being dull and somewhat boring, something you might play on a rainy Sunday with a mug of tea. However, talking to actual players revealed an interesting truth about how they saw the game. It was in fact very competitive, to the point of even being aggressive. Based on this insight, a number of different positioning directions were developed and explored in 1999 with Added Value and Brown KSDP. Each direction made use of a packaging prototype to

Before: 'World's leading word game'   After: 'Convivial mental sparring'

Figure 6.10: Scrabble re-launch reflecting essence of 'convivial mental sparring'.

Reproduced by permission of Mattel.

illustrate it. This brought the ideas to life for consumers and also allowed the design agency to develop executions in parallel with the strategy. A winning route quickly emerged that communicated the mental competition of the game by bringing the word tiles to life. Two of them were shown on the pack fighting one another for the triple word score. In addition, the brand logo itself was refreshed and given a more rounded, contemporary look. The concept and pack prototype work allowed the brand's new essence to be pinned down as 'convivial mental sparring', to capture more of the friendly mental competition that really goes on during Scrabble. The final pack design translated this into a strap line of 'Every word counts'. In the first year of launch the new packaging improved the brand's on-shelf impact and regenerated trade interest in the brand, with a resulting 35 per cent uplift in sales.

The creative leap

Brand positioning, like all strategy, is only a means to an end and not an end in itself. The 'Get real' Workout addressed the need to ensure that strategy projects are grounded in business reality and only carried out when they will drive brand mix development. The role of the positioning is to inspire and guide the teams working on developing the brand mix, both in product development and creative expression. When briefing teams and trying to make the creative leap to a great mix, several factors should be considered: 3D creative briefs, pinning down the meaning of words and not mixing up briefs with positioning.

3D creative briefs

On all too many occasions the creative briefing process leaves much to be desired, according to the people on the receiving end of it. The briefs are often badly written or in the worst cases not written at all, just delivered verbally. The old adage of 'rubbish in, rubbish out' clearly applies here and so it is no surprise that so much of the advertising you see on television is mediocre. In contrast, investing time and effort in the briefing process can pay off with better results. The idea of the 3D creative brief is to bring the consumer and the brand to life using as many different media and techniques as possible. Immersing team members in the consumer world by showing them video footage or, even better, going out to places where people are using the product will help them connect with those with whom they are trying to talk.

To present the brand itself, terms should use more than merely the onion or doughnut proposed by the agency or consultancy that worked on the project. This sort of tool is a thorough and complete 'recipe' of the brand strategy, but most internal audiences are more interested in the 'cake' that is the end result. A better way to brief teams is to 'sell the cake not the recipe'. Rather than using the whole detailed positioning tool, you can apply the same sort of visualized concept that brings to life the brand idea with a few key phrases and a set of pictures. Done well, these can end up pinned on the wall next to people's desks. You can also use examples of product prototypes or extracts from past marketing activity when the brand was strong to bring the briefing to life.

Pinning down the meaning of words

Words are incredibly subjective and if you are not careful many hours can be wasted by debating the right phrasing of a brand positioning. The task of getting the wording correct is made even harder by the fact that many brand teams are now international, with many members not having English as their first language. The line between crafting the strategy and futile tweaking is a fine one that is crossed all too easily. Experience on many projects has shown that a solution to this problem was to get teams to agree quickly on a set of words and then write a short description of what was meant by each one.

In many cases the values and personality were areas where there was the greatest potential for different interpretations of words. 'Authenticity' can conjure up images of dusty antiques for one person, whereas the meaning intended might have been being honest, real and genuine in the way you express feelings. Writing a short phrase to describe what is meant by each value, possibly accompanied by an image or two, can go a long way to explaining what is implied by each word. For example, taking the personality trait 'youthful', the following description could be given:

> Youthful: Our brand will be full of the energy, vitality and exuberance associated with being young, when you are full of hope and optimism about the future. This is more to do with a frame of mind rather than your age, and we can inspire people across different generations.

Another useful tool for pinning down the meaning of a word is to contrast it with another word that is not quite right for the brand. This pairing of words is used to show when the brand is 'on' and 'off' track. On the Cointreau brand of orange spirit, for example, the team had agreed that being 'sensual' was a key part of the brand's personality. However, research had shown that there was a limit to how far the brand could go into sensuality without losing credibility and its aura of classiness. When the brand started to show overt sexuality there was a major negative reaction and the brand went off track. This and other examples for Cointreau are shown in Table 6.6. In each case the 'on' word or phrase is taken from the positioning and contrasted with a word that is 'off' track.

Table 6.6: Examples of 'on' and 'off' positioning for Cointreau

On	Off
Sensual	Sexual
Deep	Unfathomable
Rich taste	Challenging

Not mixing up positioning and creative briefing

A common mistake made on the implementation of a brand positioning is simply to give the strategy to a creative agency and tell it to execute against the promise or essence. This approach normally fails, as it is too linear and can lead to attempts to execute the essence literally in the communication. The role of the promise and essence should be to review the creative work and ensure that this is getting and keeping the brand on track. However, the creative process is usually ignited by finding something in the positioning, often a brand truth, that sparks an executional idea. In the case of Guinness, the truth used to inspire the brand communication was the time it takes to pour a good pint of the dark stuff. This led to the advertising campaign 'Good things come to those who wait', with commercials such as 'Surfers' that was voted by consumers as their favourite of all time. This advertising helped get across the brand idea of a rewarding, enjoyable and contemporary drink, but would not have been produced by giving this desired takeout to the agency and asking for it to be executed literally.

Key takeouts

1 Brand positioning is about inspiring and guiding teams to create a competitive and coherent brand mix.
2 Most great brands are built on a truth about the product or service and a key part of the positioning process is searching for this truth. The challenge is then to look for relevant and contemporary ways of expressing this.
3 There is a risk that positioning becomes a theoretical, box-filling exercise. Emphasis should be kept on the practical application of the tool in building the brand and business.

 ## 3-part action plan

Tomorrow

For your most important brand, review the positioning strategy that you are employing and critique it using the tips and tricks suggested earlier. Is each element stripped down to the essential information or is it overloaded with words; are there any signs of the 'air-raid shelter' approach to positioning? Highlight any areas that could benefit from crafting, tightening or simplification and agree a plan to address these issues quickly and refine the strategy. Also, check that whatever format you are using, the tool answers the key questions covered in this Workout, and fill in any gaps that emerge. Finally, evaluate the positioning using the criteria of 'motivating', 'different' and 'true'.

This month

Talk to a wider set of people in the brand, business and agency teams to establish how clear an idea they have of the direction in which you are trying to take the brand. Do they all play back a consistent message when you ask them to describe the brand essence and promise, or are there different responses? Also, do they have some form of positioning that they are using to guide their brand-building efforts? Or is the strategy only a piece of paper that sits in a filing cabinet rather than being a living tool that inspires and guides them?

This year

If you undertake a positioning project during the year, seek to apply the key principles from this Workout. Ensure that the project clearly defines the role that the positioning needs to play in guiding and inspiring the mix, to ensure that the exercise is a practical and not a theoretical one. Check that the positioning directions are pushed apart enough to create truly different concepts that explore a range of possible territories for the brand. Also, take some time and money to invest in prototyping the brand ideas using product, packaging and brandcepts to bring them to life for both the consumer and yourself.

Handover

We have now completed the three Workouts that together provide the basis of developing brand strategy: focusing on a portfolio of core brands, developing a vision for each and having a positioning to keep you on track towards this. We will now move on to Part IV, which will look at how the team needs to translate this strategy into concrete actions that grow the business. The first of these will challenge you to 'Think different *and* do different' in order to help your brand stand out in an increasingly overcrowded brandscape.

BRAND ACTION

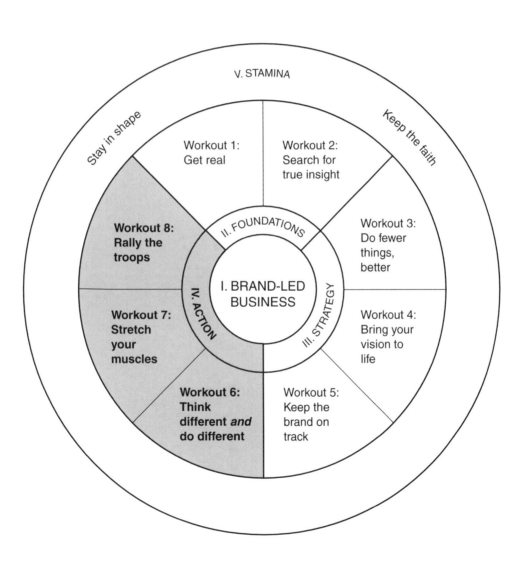

'Standing in the middle of the road is very dangerous; you get knocked down by traffic from both sides.'

Margaret Thatcher

 Headlines

Thinking different by defining a unique strategy is only the first step to standing out in today's overcrowded brandscape. The real challenge is having the courage also to *do* different by developing a disruptive brand mix. This requires teams to work on three key dimensions of differentiation: product, packaging and communication.

The benefits of being brave

More than ever, brands need to work hard to get noticed and the battle for mindspace is happening everywhere you look. Thousands of products fill up the supermarket shelf and even more crowd the virtual isles of the online grocery store. Multiple media messages hit us everywhere, from the back of a taxi to the queue at the post office. Research by the Consumers' Association for the Marketing Forum showed that 75 per cent of consumers found it hard to choose the right product or service because of the huge range available. In order to have a chance of being remembered, never mind chosen, brands need to be bold and brave to stand out from the crowd.

So, how do you go about searching for the holy grail of differentiation? Much of the work on the subject focuses on strategy and more specifically on the quest for unique benefits. However, there are several problems with relying on an all-out drive in this direction. First, unless you want to be a niche brand, you should not neglect the importance of performing against the basic, central benefits of the market, sometimes called 'market generics'. When Orange entered the UK phone market it had a narrower coverage than BT Cellnet and Vodafone. Part of its growth strategy was to develop a differentiated positioning that emphasized the emotional benefits of mobile communication. However, it also worked hard on the product to get its coverage up close to the levels of the leading brands. Without performance on this central benefit Orange was doomed to stay small for ever, whereas it is now challenging Vodafone for market leadership.

Secondly, a focus on unique benefits fails to recognize that at least half of all differentiation is created not by what you do but by how you do it. Being distinctive is not merely about crafting a clever and differentiated strategy, but also about being brave enough to follow through and execute against it. Orange had the courage to break the codes of what was a stuffy and serious market with its name and distinctive, minimalist black and orange identity. It also differentiated its product by offering features such as billing by the second. Finally, its advertising broke all the rules of the category by not showing any people using a phone but rather emphasizing the human side of communication.

Achieving true differentiation may require a change in mindset or even a change in team. In many cases brand teams claim to be committed to differentiation and demand this of their advertising and design agencies. However, these same teams have a nasty habit of chickening out when it actually comes to buying creative work that breaks the mould. They find it easier to 'step sideways not forwards' and rely on the tried-and-trusted approaches of the past. However, a breakthrough marketing mix will not happen without taking some risks and moving beyond the team's comfort zone and this means giving the creative teams freedom to experiment. The fear of losing loyal users is often used as an excuse not to rock the brand boat and it is all too easy to get consumer research to support this case. However, the risk of losing your loyal consumers through change is limited and you have to work quite hard to make them stop buying you. In contrast, it is all to easy to be so safe that you fail to recruit new users, running the risk of a slow but sure decline. This is the situation that faced one of Britain's best-known and most-loved brands, Hovis.

The Hovis story

Hovis is an example of a brand where the leadership team realized that the only way to return the business to real growth was to create a disruptive brand mix. In addition, the team decided to work on multiple dimensions of differentiation covering product, packaging and communication.

Towards the end of the 1990s a new brand development team at British Bakeries was given the challenge of revitalizing the Hovis brand. In particular, it was asked to develop a plan to build the brand's share of white bread, given that it was still locked in its historical heartland of brown bread. The team discovered a brand with incredibly rich attributes and associations, standing for natural goodness, warmth and family values. It also had real credibility and expertise in brown bread. However, the brand was also well and truly stuck in the past, a victim of its own success with advertising that was ingrained in the minds of UK consumers. When the word 'Hovis' was mentioned people immediately thought of the 'boy on a bike' advertising, first shown in 1974 but aired for an amazing 19 years. Filmed by Ridley Scott, this commercial was more like a mini-movie than an advert. Its sepia tones showed the Hovis delivery boy pushing his bike up a steep hill and then enjoying the ride back down with the reward of a Hovis sandwich for his efforts. A voiceover from a Yorkshire actor and backing from Dvorak's *New World Symphony* completed the ambiance. The end line told us that Hovis was 'As good today as it's always been.' (1).

The delicate task of the team was to separate 'heritage', equity that was key to future success, from 'history', baggage that was holding the brand down. It quickly agreed that the anchor for the brand should be goodness, still as relevant in the year 2000 as it was when the brand was created over 100 years before. The name was even rooted in the idea of being good for you, being short for *hominis vis*, meaning strength of man. However, there was a need for a radical re-interpretation of goodness for the modern British family, who had a more fragmented and unstructured approach to eating. It was no good hanging on to the past of a traditional Hovis family moment. In addition, the brand had to be radical in order to get people to re-evaluate it. The team needed to take a deep breath and make some brave moves.

A new communication campaign was developed with agency BMP that could not have been further away from the boy and his bike. A *Simpsons*-style cartoon family was used to show 'real' kids talking about how all they ate was rubbish, yet enjoying a Hovis sandwich (Figure 7.1). The tag line of 'Get something good inside' was true to the brand's essence, but had a much more modern, active feel to it. This advertising broke all the codes of Hovis advertising and achieved its aim of getting the brand on to consumers' radar screen, especially among younger families. Nevertheless, it was one thing to get people to the supermarket shelf but another altogether to get them to pick up a pack and buy it. How could the team ensure there wasn't a disconnect between advertising and packaging?

On packaging the team was also brave, using photos of food such as baked beans to enliven the packs in place of the traditional Hovis graphics (Figure 7.2). Again this was loyal to the brand's values, by showing the sort of good, wholesome food that you would want to eat with Hovis, but the way these values were executed was totally new. The design had the desired effect of getting the brand noticed and even talked about. Following the launch in July 2001 the company received 2500 consumer letters. Some people

Figure 7.1: The new Hovis family used in communication.

Reproduced by permission of British Bakeries.

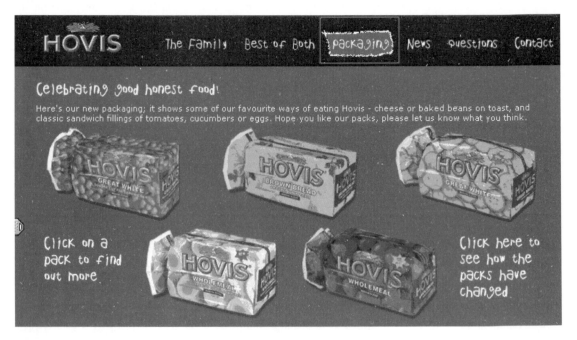

Figure 7.2: Disruptive new Hovis packaging.

Reproduced by permission of British Bakeries.

loved the idea, applauding its originality and creativity. Others hated it and criticized the brand's search for modernity. However, what mattered most was that the brand was connecting with consumers and breaking out of its straitjacket.

The final piece of the puzzle was the product and a way to make a breakthrough in the white bread market. Here, the team did what many great brands do and created a trade-off: it delivered the goodness of brown bread in a white sliced loaf. The product was aptly named 'Best of Both' and gave mums what they had been waiting for: a way to 'smuggle' the goodness of brown bread into food their children would want to eat.

The results from the re-launch confirmed the benefits of being brave. Sales volumes in 2001 were up over 20 per cent after a 10 per cent increase the year before and the brand now has a retail value of almost £200 million. It has become the leading white sliced loaf, achieving the objective of moving away from its exclusive association with brown bread. Brand image ratings have improved, both on the core image dimension of 'good for you' and on 'good at white bread'. Penetration has increased, with a particular increase among younger families.

 ## 5-minute workout

Pick a couple of creative briefs that you are working on at the moment. Are you giving the agencies as much freedom as Hovis did to push the boundaries of expression and create true differentiation? Or are you being brave in the strategy and cautious in the execution? If you were to 'do a Hovis' on your brand and revolutionize product, packaging and communication, what would this look like and what results would you expect? Think about the barriers that are stopping you being as bold as the Hovis team and how you might break them down.

Four dimensions of differentiation

Doing different in addition to merely thinking different relies not on the discovery of a single killer benefit but rather on building several dimensions of differentiation. Standing out becomes an ongoing process rather than a one-off exercise. This is especially true when the speed of competitive response is so fast, leaving you a limited window of opportunity to exploit an idea. Building multiple dimensions of differentiation makes it much harder for competitors to copy the brand, as they have to replicate and configure many different elements (Figure 7.3).

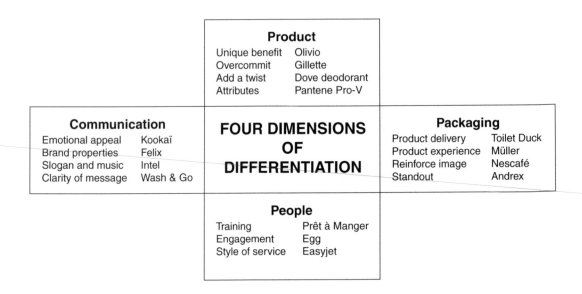

Figure 7.3: The four dimensions of differentiation.

We will now look in more detail at the three dimensions that were introduced in the Hovis story: product, packaging and communication. A fourth dimension, people, will be discussed in more detail in a later Workout, 'Rally the troops'.

The product dimension

Behind many great brands there is, of course, a great product. Although clever marketing can persuade people to try a brand once, if the product or service does not deliver then re-purchase and loyalty are unlikely to follow. There are several ways of working on the product dimension introduced in the last Workout that we will now look at in more detail: being unique, overcommitting, adding a twist and finding a magic ingredient.

Being unique

The ultimate source of differentiation is to have a product that delivers a relevant benefit that no other brand can match. The olive oil spread Olivio, from Bertolli, has built a strong and differentiated positioning by selling the benefit of longevity, supported by being part of a Mediterranean diet based on olive oil. Although retailers quickly launched copy-cat olive oil spreads, their image rating on 'Helps you live a longer life' (3 per cent) was miles away from that for Olivio (61 per cent). However, although the strategy of focusing on longevity was part of the success, a huge factor was also the way in which this benefit was communicated. With limited support a share of only 0.6 per cent of the £500 million margarine market had been achieved several years after the 1992 launch. The brand really took off when the team started using communication to bring alive the 'Olivio way of life'. This entertaining and amusing campaign portrayed old people in a sunny, Mediterranean setting enjoying fun and games at a ripe old age. One of the tag lines, 'Club 18–130', summarized the Bertolli philosophy of life. Olivio's approach to health was one of light-hearted seduction, in contrast to the more hard-core message of brands like Flora. People buying Olivio like the product but they love the brand world it portrays. The new campaign helped more than treble the share to 2.0 per cent while maintaining a price premium over own label (2).

Overcommitting

If you can't find and own a unique benefit, or believe that this will not lead to a sufficiently large market share, the next possibility is to overdeliver on a core benefit. This has the advantage of allowing you to compete in the centre ground of the market, giving you a shot at offering what most consumers want to buy most of the time. Gillette has consistently overdelivered on the core benefit of close shaving by investing hundreds of millions of dollars in developing truly superior shavers. Importantly, it has launched wave after wave of differentiation starting with the Sensor, following with the Sensor Excell and then the Mach 3. Each of these innovations raises even higher the bar on the core benefit and makes it harder for competition to respond.

Delivering more of the core benefit is a hard and expensive battle to fight, but when you win you normally end up with the market-leading position. Over years of research, Kimberly Clark found that the Andrex product mix of 'soft, strong and long' was the ideal combination of benefits in the toilet tissue market. By delivering more on each of these core benefits, Andrex has built a strong central position that is hard to attack. This is shown by the limited inroads made by P&G's launch of Charmin in the UK, despite heavy investment.

Adding a twist

Few companies are lucky enough to have a truly superior product. An easier source of differentiation may be adding a 'twist' to the product, while still offering a good level of delivery on the core benefits of the market. Watch out here to ensure that you do perform acceptably on the core benefit, otherwise few people will buy your product, no matter how attractive your new twist. Professor Kevin Keller calls this offering a 'point of parity' in addition to a 'point of difference'. His research has shown that it is the failure to offer a point of parity that often trips up new product launches (3). For example, Dove's entry into the deodorant market needs to emphasize efficacy against sweat and odour if people are to trust it enough to switch from their current brand. Clearly the skin mildness benefit still needs to be present, to avoid diluting the total brand idea, but the volume needs turning up on the efficacy message to establish a point of parity against existing brands.

In service businesses the challenge is not to add a single twist but rather to add as many as possible. Virgin Airlines' planes aren't faster or more punctual and like everyone they try to offer excellent on-board service. However, the little touches like massages and video games together build uniqueness. Amazon's personal recommendations, reader reviews and super-reliable delivery add up to create a differentiated service for that company.

Finding a magic ingredient

In a busy world with too many messages competing for too little attention, product attributes can be a powerful way for brands to cut through and achieve differentiation. Done well, a product feature can be very effective at short-cutting the process of communicating superiority versus competition. Pantene's benefit of hair health was quickly copied and indeed became the core benefit in the shampoo market, but it has built strong awareness of the Pro-Vitamin B5 'magic' ingredient through consistent communication on pack and in advertising. The thickness of Domestos bleach or Tetley's round tea bags are other examples where product attributes deliver core benefits in a differentiating way, rather than offering new benefits all together.

Where possible, features should deliver real and meaningful benefits and avoid the '0.1 per cent' trick. This involves adding a drop of an ingredient to a product to allow a claim to be made, even though this makes no difference to the product experience. Eventually consumers are clever enough to figure out that such product features are a con and they will not pay a premium for them. The strongest brands tend to be those where product features do enhance the experience in use, even if in only a small way, such as Dove's ¼ moisturizing cream.

The packaging dimension

Design is an incredibly rich source of differentiation that has the benefit of being present with the consumer all the way through the life of the product, versus the more ephemeral nature of communication. The design dimension can help product delivery, enhance the product experience, reinforce the brand image and create standout (Figure 7.4).

Helping product delivery (Toilet Duck)

Enhancing product experience (Müller)

Reinforcing brand imagery (Gold Blend)

Creating standout (Andrex)

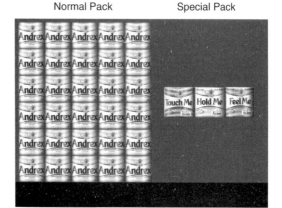

Figure 7.4: Packaging as a differentiator.

Toilet Duck packshot reproduced by permission of Düring AG; Müller fruit corner packshot reproduced by permission of Müller Dairy UK; Nescafé Gold Blend packshot reproduced by permission of Nescafé; Andrex packshot reproduced by permission of Kimberley Clark Limited.

Helping product delivery

Packaging can be used to help in delivering the product to provide extra benefits. For example, Toilet Duck's success owes much to the bendy-shaped neck that enables you to get to those hard-to-reach places where germs lurk under the rim. The pack shape and name have also inspired the creation of a duck character that has starred in advertising for more than a decade, putting personality and warmth into a fairly mundane product.

Enhancing the product experience

Packaging can transform the experience of consuming a product. Müller has revolution-ized the UK yoghurt market, achieving a market-leading 40 per cent share and building a billion-pound brand. A big part of its success has been its revolutionary 'split pot' with separate compartments for yoghurt and fruit. Who would have thought that someone could charge people a premium and get them to mix the fruit and yoghurt rather than this being done in the factory? What Müller realized is that people love to 'do it their own way' when it comes to food, choosing to eat the combination of ingredients in way that suits them. In addition, the brand delivered a generous portion of rich, creamy yoghurt and thick, tasty fruit at a time when other brands had been taking out ingredients and cutting pack sizes to cut costs.

Another great example of pack format transforming the product experience is the Pringles tube, before the launch of which all crisps were sold in plastic bags. The tube not only looks different, it allows the product to be stacked in a way that preserves the integrity of the potato chips and stops them from breaking. The pack format has even inspired the communication idea 'Once you pop, you can't stop!'

Reinforcing brand image

As in the case of Pringles, structural packaging can be a superb way of making your product look completely different and reinforce the desired brand image. Nescafé has used packaging structure with huge success to reinforce the premium nature and taste values of its Gold Blend coffee. This has been a key factor in differentiating versus retailers' own brands. As with Gillette, Nescafé has not stopped at one pack innovation, starting out with a square cross-section pack but then following up with an even more distinctively shaped pack in the last couple of years. As another example, Häagen Dazs created a whole new category of 'super-premium' ice cream in Europe by selling product in 500ml pots instead of the conventional big tubs used by other brands.

Beyond merely looking good, the structure of packaging can be used to make a product appear more appealing and so drive purchase at the point of sale. Sticking with the world of ice cream, Carte d'Or has finally made inroads in the UK after several false starts with a product range called Artisinal that has many interesting ingredients and swirls of sauce that you can view in the product. The use of a transparent plastic tub ensures that shoppers can see the product differentiation in the shop and so they are more likely to pick it up and buy it. No amount of strategy refinement would have helped Carte d'Or, it was the packaging innovation that made the difference.

Creating standout

Even with no budget for structural packaging changes, there is still the possibility of using pack graphics to create differentiation and boost sales. Kimberly Clark used this route to support the 2001 re-launch of Andrex toilet tissue, which sought to reinforce the core benefits of thickness, absorbance and softness. The company asked design agency Brown KSDP for ideas to make the packaging work harder at point of sale to create impact. In a category that was heavily promoted with on-pack flashes, something special had to be created to cut-through. The agency came up with several creative ideas, including one that was way outside the comfort zone. The proposal was to replace the brand name in the logo with one of three phrases that made up the re-launch communication idea: 'Feel me', 'Hold me' or 'Touch me'. The brand name would appear, but only in small text at the bottom of the pack. The client's initial reaction was understandably a sharp intake of breath and a slightly less polite version of 'bugger me'. After all, the pack broke the cardinal rule of brand identity never to play around with your logo. However, it delivered massively against the brief of creating impact, as the Category Director at Kimberly Clark, Joe Bromilow, explained:

> The solution worked in a very simple but effective way. At first glance, the shopper sees the normal pack. However, the new words replacing Andrex in the logo cause a second glance and create real cut-through. This is one of the few times that I have experienced shoppers talking about packaging whilst shopping!

All credit to the team for having the courage to back the idea. The company is now reaping the success of the increased effectiveness of the pack at point of sale, achieved at a cost of almost zero.

The communication dimension

Communication can be one of the most powerful weapons in the battle for differentiation. It is here that the brand truly comes to life and expresses its values and personality. Ways of using this dimension include winning hearts, creating properties and hitting harder.

Creating emotional appeal

The growth of the Kookaï chain of clothing stores in France owed much to being brave in communication. Two friends, Jean Lou Teper and Philippe de Hesdin, created the business in 1983. They were entrepreneurs more than marketing people and their brief to BBDO's Paris office was not much more sophisticated than 'surprise us'. The brand needed to be disruptive given the small budgets available and the use of posters as the main media. The campaign communicated a form of 'girl power' years before pop group the Spice Girls claimed this as a rallying call. Campaigns portrayed the power that Kookaï girls had over their men, who were miniaturized and flushed down the loo or used to keep toes apart to allow nails to be painted! This communication created a distinctive personality for the brand that was a key part of helping the brand grow sales by 70 per cent between 1994 and 1998 to about £80 million.

Brand properties

Brand properties, such as characters, slogans and jingles, can be a major source of differentiation when they are executed well and with consistency over time. These properties are keys that can unlock a set of benefits and associations. Hear the Intel four-note refrain and a string of associations to do with processing power, leadership and technology come to mind. And a cat called Felix shows just how valuable an asset a brand property can be.

Quaker introduced Felix the cat to the world in 1989, when its brand of cat food had a tiny 6 per cent share and was in danger of being de-listed. The brand leader at the time was Pedigree's Whiskas, which portrayed squeaky clean, tidy, purring cats. The voice of the brand reassured you that '9 out of 10 owners say their cats prefer Whiskas'. The Felix team and its agency BMP decided that they had to be brave enough to break the category rules. They built on an insight that most people didn't have perfect, preened cats like the ones in Whiskas' world. Felix was an animated cat who got up to tricks and had a mischievous grin (Figure 7.5). Out went the voiceovers about meaty chunks and goodness, in came feline fun and games. The tag line summed up the idea by saying that 'Cats like Felix like Felix'.

Figure 7.5: Felix the cat brand property.

Reproduced by permission of Nestlé Purina PetCare (UK) Ltd.

The property helped make the brand more loveable at the same time as strengthening ratings on quality. Other dimensions of differentiation were also tapped into. The packaging featured paw prints not quality seals, new product variants used names like 'Rascal's Reward' and avoided fancy foody words, and Felix became the star of the website. A Felix screen saver spread by viral marketing to be present on hundreds of thousands of computers. Over the 1990s Felix grew share to end up at 26 per cent, taking leadership from Whiskas which fell from 30 to 25 per cent (4).

The challenge with a strong property like the Andrex puppy or the PG Tips chimps is how to keep the communication fresh and interesting. The risk is that instead of triggering positive associations, the property causes people to switch off. The trick is to find new and different ways of using it. Over the years the Andrex campaign has been kept fresh by showing the puppies in many different roles. They have played with children, cavorted through pink feathers and rubbed noses with other cute animals.

Clarity of message

In 1987 Unilever was first to market with a 2-in-1 shampoo called Dimension. P&G's Wash & Go was launched a year later and took a 12 per cent share versus Dimension's 3 per cent. The biggest difference was not in the fundamental concept, beautiful hair with less fuss, it was in the simplicity of the communication. Dimension claimed to be 'A shampoo so good you don't need a conditioner', which left consumers bemused. Wash & Go simply said 'Shampoo and Conditioner, in one'. You might have hated those commercials with images of bottles splashing down from lockers, but they did get the message across.

The people dimension

Clearly, in a service business the people are the brand and the brand is the people. Investing time, effort and money can pay off in a differentiated brand proposition, with some of the specific angles being training, engagement and service style.

Training

Every company will emphasize the training it gives its people, but in some cases this is a token gesture. The actual delivery is hit and miss, with the quality level variable. In places like Prêt à Manger and Starbucks the story is very different, and an almost fanatical attention to detail and consistency flow through into thorough and ongoing training. For example, at Prêt everyone learns how to make the perfect sandwich, including management hires. In addition, there are a number of little tricks people are taught that make for a friendly and informal eating experience, such as the being trained to put money directly in the customer's hand, not on the counter top.

Engagement

We will cover the issue of engagement in more detail in Workout Eight, 'Rally the troops'. The main point is that people who are genuinely engaged with the mission and vision of the business tend to deliver a higher quality of service to customers. People working at Egg, for example, do seem to feel as if they are part of an adventure that is all about re-inventing the world of financial services in the UK. They buy into the company's values of informality, honesty and innovation and this comes across when they talk to you. The human dimension is obviously key for Egg as it is a virtual bank with no branches.

Service style

The tone, style and personality of the people in a business can also be a source of differentiation, not so much what they do but rather how they do it. Take British Airways, Air

France and easyJet, for example. When it works well, BA's service exudes the polite, correct aspect of the British character, with pilots apologizing profusely for turbulence or delays caused by air traffic control. Air France hostesses are very French. They tend to be chic, well dressed and often a bit superior! But my favourite is easyJet. The company's service concept is designed to drive out cost. There are no tickets (you use your credit card to check in), no assigned seat numbers (first on gets first pick), no inferior on-board food. Nevertheless, far from feeling cheap the whole thing is refreshingly simple, down to earth and informal. The staff call you by your first name and the orange sleeveless shirts worn by staff almost look cool.

 ## Key takeouts

1 Strategy can only get you so far in the journey towards differentiation. How you execute the strategy is just as important.
2 Many brands fail to differentiate themselves because the teams managing them lack the courage to produce a truly distinctive brand mix.
3 Not changing out of fear of losing loyal consumers leads to the risk of a worse and potentially fatal future in which you fail to attract new users, the lifeblood of any brand.
4 The best way to differentiate is to use all four dimensions of product, packaging, people and communication.

 ## 3-part action plan

Tomorrow

Start by reviewing your brand mix against the four dimensions of differentiation. How well are product, pack, people and communication being leveraged to make your brand stand out from the competition in the marketplace, not merely on paper? Where are there opportunities to build in more points of difference?

This month

Review the creative briefs on your live brand projects to see if they are written in a way that gives the teams working on them the opportunity to stretch the envelope of the brand and push outside your comfort zone. Are you asking for differentiation, yet at the same time putting so many constraints on your agencies as to make this an impossible task? On at least one project, commit to liberating the creative team as much as possible and challenge them to do something that scares the pants off you. You can start small by choosing a promotion or piece of direct marketing, for example, but don't fall into the trap of falling back on a consumer test to reassure you.

This year

Over the year review the team you have in place and ask yourself how capable its members are of helping you create differentiation for your brand. Are they challenging you and pushing the boundaries of execution, or relying on yesterday's tried-and-trusted recipes? You should have at least some challengers in the team who are looking for new and better ways of achieving relevant differentiation. Also, review the agencies you use for advertising, design and other areas of the mix. How good are they at helping you achieve a mix that allows your brand to get noticed among all the noise and confusion of the marketplace? Are you getting the best creative resource on your brand, capable of building the emotional appeal, brand properties and packaging that can set you apart and support a price premium? If you are not, then the first place to look is probably yourself and the way you manage the agency. Are you showing courage in the search for true differentiation in the marketing mix or, like so many people, only thinking different on paper?

 **Handover**

We now have a good overview of the brand actions that can translate a strategy into a mix with the potential to grow the business. We will now review in more depth what is potentially one of the best ways a brand can build both image and sales: brand extension. As portfolios become more focused and the surviving brands are expected to take up more of the demands for growth from the business, brand stretch is one of the key actions for teams today. 'Stretching your muscles' will look at how brand extension can be a driver of profitable growth, but also at the many risks that it presents and how to avoid them.

Workout Seven: Stretch your muscles

CHAPTER 8

'The opportunities of man are only limited by his imagination.
But so few have imagination that there are ten thousand fiddlers for every one composer.'

Charles. F. Kettering

 ## Headlines

Brand extension can be one of the best sources of profitable growth for a brand. Big, bold ideas that offer a true point of difference can attract new users or create new usage occasions without the cost of developing a new brand. Extensions also have the potential to help rejuvenate a brand's imagery, as shown by examples like the iMac from Apple or the new Volkswagen Beetle. However, too many extensions are mere fiddles that eat up money and resources without delivering any real difference versus existing products. These dwarf products simply cannibalize existing sales, leading to a fragmented and weakened brand.

Why extensions fail

Branding theory is often used to explain why extensions fail and there is a great deal of explaining to do: 72 per cent of them flop, according to an Ernst & Young survey done in 1998. Stretching too far from the equity of the 'mother brand' is the favourite excuse. However, the real explanations are much more simple and down to earth. Often the product simply adds nothing new and better to make people put it on their regular shopping list. The novelty factor might make people try something once, but this effect is very short-lived. Enigma, Guinness's attempt to get out of stout and into lager, didn't flop because it stretched the brand too far. It failed because it had no real advantage over the plethora of other lagers in the UK. In contrast, Yamaha sells large numbers of Clavinova electronic pianos because the product is excellent. Consumers don't worry about the fact that the brand has stretched from motorbikes to musical instruments.

Even if the product does deliver, it may not justify the price positioning, leading to a poor value equation and no re-purchase. The failure of My Home, Persil's home laundry service, was less to do with brand stretch and more to do with the price tag of several pounds per shirt ironed.

Another key reason for failed extensions is that they don't even get the chance to prove how good they are because there is a lack of investment support. Many new products are not big enough ideas to get a lot of money put behind them. This means that they end up with a limited amount of advertising and promotion and so initial sales are slow. This leads to retailers de-listing the new product and a further decline in sales, which in turn means that there is less brand support, and on it goes. To have a good chance of success, teams need the imagination and ambition to stretch the brand into new areas that offer a real plus for the consumer, with the brand and business-building potential to justify heavy marketing support.

Building business, building brands

Building business

The primary motivation behind brand stretch should always be to deliver *profitable business growth* (Figure 8.1). There are several different ways in which a brand extension can create business growth: attracting new users, creating new usage occasions and premium pricing.

New users

New users who are unlikely to buy the current products can be attracted into the brand via an extension. Developing a new product is justified when the additional benefits that need to be offered to bring in new users cannot be delivered without compromising the performance of the existing product. Shampoo Head & Shoulders grew 10 per cent by introducing a frequent wash version for the increasing number of people with slight dandruff who thought that the classic product was too harsh. They were attracted by a product with a lower level of active ingredient, more conditioning qualities and less medicinal perfume. If this combination of changes had been made to the original product it would have turned off loyal users, who liked the idea of a powerful, no-nonsense dandruff remedy. Hence an extension rather than a core product upgrade was the right choice.

New usage occasions

New occasions can also be a source of growth for brand stretch, often resulting from a team having the imagination to think about the market in a broader sense. Pampers has started

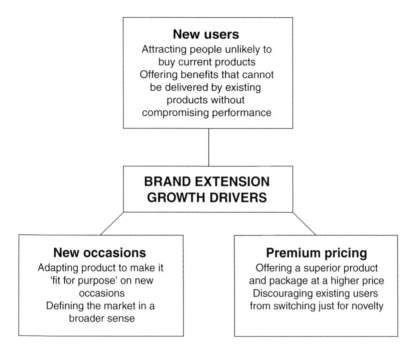

Figure 8.1: Brand extension growth drivers.

to evolve from being a nappy to a baby care brand through the successful launch of baby wipes. The company has followed this up with the introduction of disposable paper bibs and changing mats. KitKat Chunky grew share by 45 per cent by taking the brand into eating occasions where a more substantial and filling snack was required (1).

Premium pricing

Premium price positioning can be an excellent source of incremental profit, by offering a superior product and package at a higher price, as Nescafé has done with its Gold Blend coffee. The higher price has the advantage of discouraging existing users from switching just for the novelty factor, with people needing to have a real interest in the new offer to be willing to pay more for it.

Results from Gillette shaving products confirm the business-building effect that extensions can have, transforming a company that was in threat of decline in the face of competition from cheap plastic razors in the 1980s. Starting with the Sensor in 1992, Gillette launched a new shaver that raised the performance standard in the market, attracting users back from disposables and persuading them to pay a price premium. Rather than resting

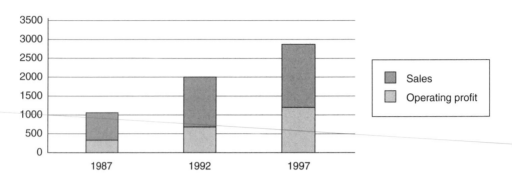

Figure 8.2: Growth in Gillette sales and profitability.

on its laurels, further waves of product innovation kept both sales and profitability growing (Figure 8.2). In particular, Sensor for Women in 1992 brought in a whole wave of new female users and created a business worth several million dollars. The Mach 3 is the latest addition, with the cartridges priced at a 50 per cent premium versus the Sensor Excel. This new product was the result of a $1 billion investment in R&D, with a further $300 million spent on first-year marketing in the US alone (2).

Building image

Beyond the primary benefit of business building, extensions do also have the potential to *build brand image*, by reinforcing or helping create the desired positioning. New products done well are a sign of brand vitality, creating a sense of dynamism and innovation, in contrast to brands that are static and offer the same old products as they always have. However, a common mistake is to assume that the launch of a new extension will automatically have a positive 'halo' effect on the existing products; this rarely or never happens. The brand itself may benefit from an improved image and so be more capable of launching other new products. However, if the existing products still look, feel and act the same, they are unlikely to see their fortunes miraculously change overnight. Take Chrysler's launch of the striking PT Cruiser retro-styled car. As one observer noted: 'So far, there is little indication that the craze over the PT is sparking enthusiasm in the U.S. for other Chysler-brand vehicles' (3).

One new product, no matter how hot, is not enough to reverse the fortunes of a company. Rather, the new product needs to stimulate and inspire a renewed mix and product offering

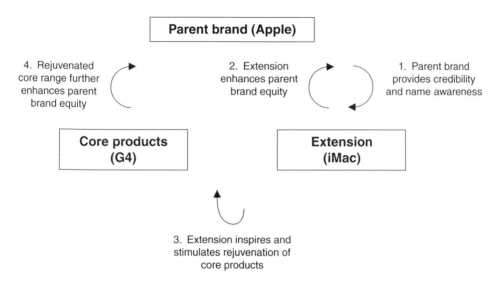

Figure 8.3: Brand equity effects of extensions.

on the core products (Figure 8.3), as has been the case with Apple. The company's launch of the iMac in 1998 was the first of a stream of new products that delivered innovation in design and features. After the iMac came the iBook, a revolutionary laptop computer. Then followed the new powerful Power Mac G4 desktop and iPod, Apple's entry into the MP3 market (Figure 8.4). The iMac kicked off the return of Apple led from the top by Steve Jobs. Furthermore, it was not a one-hit wonder where Apple got lucky. It was the result of the company getting back in touch with the core values that made it great in the first place, as described by Pascal Cagni, Vice President and General Manager, Apple EMEA:

> Apple had always stood for innovation and ease of use but we lost our way in the early 1990s trying to play catch up with the PC makers. iMac was the start of the revival of the brand and business when we re-focused on what we stood for, what made us different from the competition. We stopped making beige boxes like the other guys and started doing what we are best at, pushing the boundaries forward with innovative, appealing and relevant products.

Bringing together brand and business building

The rating on each of the business- and brand-building dimensions can be plotted on a simple matrix (Figure 8.5) to identify the potential of the new product, as illustrated by looking at the history of extensions on the Gillette brand:

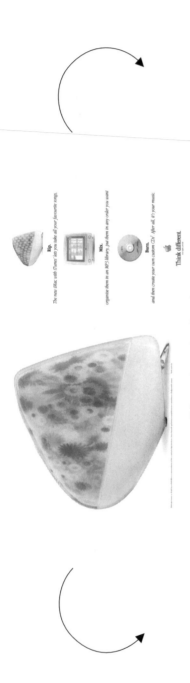

Inspires re-invention of core product
(laptop computer): iBook

iMac = brand extension

Inspires creation of new product:
iPod MP3 payer

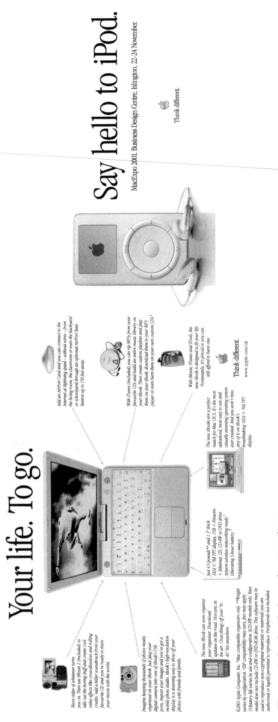

Figure 8.4: Apple brand extensions.

Reproduced by permission of Apple Computer, Inc. Apple, the Apple logo, Macintosh, Mac, iBook, iMac, MacOS, PowerBook and Power Mac are either registered trademarks or trademarks of Apple. © 2002 Apple Computer, Inc.

BRAND IMAGE BUILD

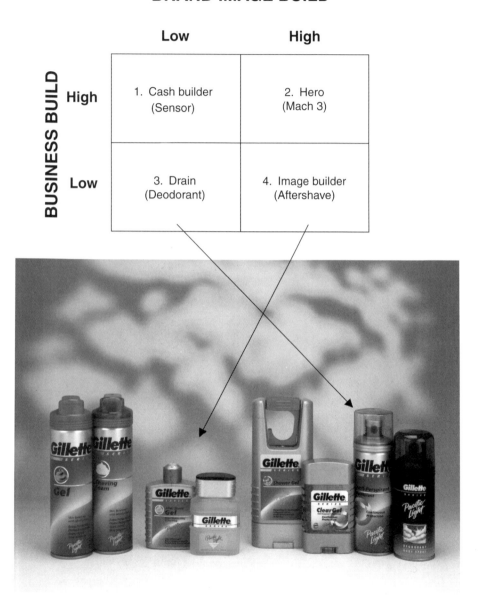

Figure 8.5: Brand- and business-building matrix for Gillette.

Path shots reproduced by permission of The Gillette Company.

1 *The Sensor razor system is now a 'cash builder'* that accounts for a good chunk of profit, but doesn't do much for the brand image, having been superseded by the new-generation Sensor Excel and Mach 3. The temptation may be to try to tweak and modify these projects or products to get them 'on strategy', but a better option is just to let them 'tick along' and make money so that you can focus resources on hero products.

2 *The Mach 3 is a 'hero'* product that dramatizes the brand positioning, in this case shaving performance, and at the same time generates profitable and significant business growth. The Mach 3 alone is now a billion-dollar business in its own right.

3 *Aerosol deodorant is a 'drain'* because it eats up resources and has a limited impact on either brand image or business growth. The deodorant market is highly competitive and entering it takes significant budget away from the core shaving business. In addition, the added value of the brand for consumers is limited as the brand is stretching outside of its area of expertise of shaving and not bringing anything new. The clear gel version perhaps has more chance of success as at least the format is different from the norm.

4 *Aftershave lotion is an 'image builder'* that is small in terms of incremental profit, yet does something positive for Gillette by creating a sense of its being a high-performance 'male grooming' brand. The product is still linked to the brand's core competence of shaving expertise. However, this is the most risky type of extension in many ways, as it runs the danger of eating up resources without delivering the image-building effect that would justify this. Small profit ideas usually end up being small in every sense: sales, marketing support and consumer awareness. They have to be very powerful in image terms to have an impact on the brand as a whole.

The Bacardi Breezer story

Bacardi Breezer shows just how big a contribution an extension can make in building both the business and the brand, with sales a staggering seven times the size of the core 'Carta Blanca' rum (Figure 8.6). This has been achieved by leveraging all three of the brand extension growth levers: new users, new occasions and premium pricing.

Breezer has attracted new users by delivering a more contemporary product, pack and communication campaign. The product developed is a refreshing, ready-to-drink mix of real Bacardi rum, fruit juice and spring water that still packs a punch, with the 5.4 per cent alcohol content being above that of beers like Budweiser. The real spirit and alcoholic edge also helps support a 25 per cent price premium over beer, which generates funds for marketing support. The bottle uses the codes of premium-packaged lager, giving it a

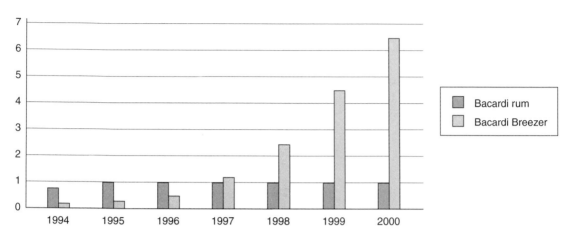

Figure 8.6: Business-building effect of Bacardi Breezer.

younger and more informal feel than classic spirits (Figure 8.7). This pack format also takes the brand into new occasions, whether it be holding the bottle on the dance floor or more regular in-home drinking; you are likely to get through a six-pack of Breezer in the fridge more quickly than a bottle of Carta Blanca rum in the cupboard.

The success of Breezer also shows the importance of stamina when launching new products. Several years of in-market learning were needed before sales really took off, as the Marketing Director Maurice Doyle, who launched the brand as Senior Brand Manager in 1994, explains:

> We learned and evolved as we went. As a private company we have slightly longer time frames and once we have decided to do something we have patience and stick with it.

By the mid-1990s Breezer had grown to about 300 000 cases. At one-third the size of the mother brand, this was already much more successful than most extensions. However, the team had bigger ambitions and set itself a stretchy target of being as big as Budweiser. This vision forced the company make big, bold moves, the first of which was to grow 'on trade' distribution aggressively in Britain's 130 000 clubs and bars. At the time Breezer was hardly present in this sector, reflecting a relative lack of sales force here. Nevertheless, without a strong presence in this sector the team knew that the brand would not achieve the sales levels for which they were aiming. It would also lack the street credibility and aspirational values that are critical for a successful spirits brand. A new, smaller 275ml

Figure 8.7: Bacardi Breezer product range.

Reproduced by permission of Bacardi & Company Limited. BACARDI, BREEZER and the Bat Device are registered trademarks of Bacardi & Company Limited.

beer-bottle-shaped pack was developed to get the unit price down to a more attractive level for buying in a bar. A dedicated, younger and cooler sales force was also recruited to begin the long, hard task of getting Breezer distributed and promoted. These efforts have paid off well, with distribution of 69 per cent only several points behind Budweiser.

The other key factor that helped create the explosion of sales in the late 1990s was the communication campaign based on the idea of 'There's Latin spirit in every one'. This has a double message. First, there is real Bacardi rum in the bottle, providing authenticity and credibility versus other pre-mixed 'alcopop' drinks like Hooch alcoholic lemonade. In addition, the advertising dramatized that in all Anglo-Saxons there is a more sociable, extrovert, party side. The campaign showed people in formal situations daydreaming about their extravagant, Latin-inspired exploits from the night before. This showed a more energetic, youthful and contemporary side to the brand that attracted younger drinkers (Figure 8.8). The 'nice on the outside, naughty on the inside' idea was taken to a new level with the arrival of the tomcat in 2000. The cat seems like a loveable rogue who is almost a man in a cat's body, jumping in the air when a goal is scored and chatting up girls. The

Figure 8.8: Bacardi Breezer communication.

Reproduced by permission of Bacardi & Company Limited.

clever trick is that the tomcat can do things that normal people could not be shown doing in advertising as it would lack credibility or simply be illegal! The campaign won the award for Marketing Effectiveness Campaign of the Year in 2001.

In addition to building the business, Breezer inspired a re-invention of the core Carta Blanca rum mix. The company had been trying to give Carta Blanca a more masculine image. Black and white advertising portrayed Cuban boxers from the 1950s to communicate the authentic roots of the brand. The success of Breezer helped remind the team that Bacardi was a 'good-time brand', compared to most other spirit brands that are cold, edgy and hard to understand. New advertising with the idea of 'Welcome to the Latin quarter' seeks to inject the same youthful energy and party spirit into the core rum. In addition, Carta Blaca is benefiting from the new on-trade sales force recruited to promote Breezer.

 ## 5-minute workout

Take the latest brand extension project you are working on and compare it to the Bacardi Breezer story. Does your planned extension do as good a job of attracting new users or creating new usage occasions for the brand, or is it doomed to be a dwarf? Is it new and different enough to justify a premium price and so generate funds for marketing investment or will it cannibalize sales without enhancing profitability?

Elastic brands

The new brand button often gets hit before the opportunities for brand stretch have been fully explored, leading to fragmentation and eventually the need to re-focus the portfolio. When considering brand stretch, it is important to do this on two different dimensions:

- *Functional stretch*: this dimension is to do with the delivery of different benefits that require different product features and functionality. The key issue is one of competence to offer a certain product or service under the brand in question. In the case of Tesco, how credible is it that a supermarket could offer reliable financial services? A decade ago you might have said that this was a big stretch, but now Tesco is one of the country's most respected and trusted companies and many consumers are voting 'yes' by moving their savings and loans there.
- *Emotional stretch*: this dimension is to with the emotional associations and personality of a market or segment. The key issue here is about the feel, tone and style needed to compete effectively. Price positioning is often another important consideration, as the emotions attached to cheap, mainstream and premium-priced segments are very different, even if the underlying basics of functionality are the same. Using Tesco again, it might be able to buy diamonds and turn them into great-looking jewellery, but the emotional stretch from what Tesco stands for today would be very far.

Considering the emotional and functional dimensions gives you an idea of how big the stretch is from the core brand to the new product or service (Figure 8.9). The bigger the stretch from the core, the harder it will be for the brand to pull off the extension successfully. When the stretch is big, a sub-brand or new brand may be needed to give the new launch the best chance of success. This is particularly the case for emotional stretch, as this requires a different personality versus the core brand and is hard to achieve without a new name. Bacardi may not have had the same success with a product called 'Bacardi, Lime and Soda' as it did using the Breezer sub-brand. The product had the same 'family name' of Bacardi, but a new 'first name' of Breezer that could take on a slightly different personality. The stretch for Toyota into luxury cars was even bigger, both functionally and emotionally, leading to the creation of the Lexus brand.

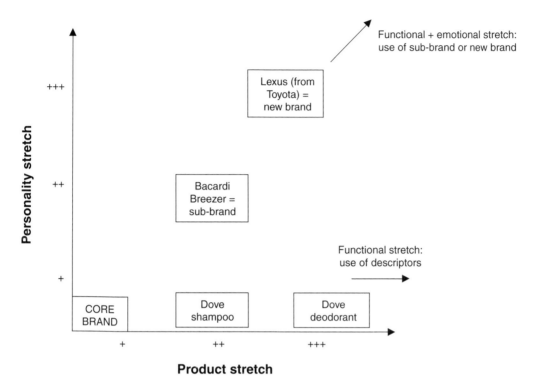

Figure 8.9: Brand stretch analysis.

In contrast, functional stretch is more an issue of providing reassurance and reasons to believe that the brand is competent to offer the new product. Dove going from skin cleansing into shampoo does require the brand to persuade consumers that the shampoo leaves their hair looking fantastic. However, the personality of Dove works well in the new product area and the emotional stretch is limited, so a descriptive name works.

Clearly, not all brands are as elastic as one another and this difference can be explained by a series of factors: suppleness from stretching before, open or closed name, the balance of emotional versus functional equity and core product performance.

Suppleness from stretching before

Stretching a brand is not unlike stretching a muscle, in that the more you do it the easier it gets. A brand like Dove that has stretched into new areas such as deodorant and now shampoo has progressively increased its footprint and with each new launch it becomes less surprising that it should launch a new product.

Open or closed name

The benefit of a made-up name with no inherent meaning, such as Yahoo!, is that it may be easier to propose new product offerings that stretch from the core. In contrast, Freeserve's descriptive name has not helped it to stretch beyond its core business of free Internet access into more profitable fee paying services. An even more extreme example is British Gas's attempt to sell electricity, which is obviously not helped by its name.

Emotional versus functional equity

Brands that are deeply rooted in a functional promise, such as Head & Shoulders dandruff shampoo, will find it harder to stretch beyond their core area of expertise. In contrast, brands that are rich in emotional values and not associated with a specific functional benefit are easier to stretch over multiple product areas. Axe/Lynx has taken the idea of giving a man pulling power to get the girl from just smelling good with body spray into shaving, shower gel and hair styling.

Product performance

As one general manager at P&G would always say, 'A sick mother cannot give birth to a healthy child.' If a brand is not performing in its core area, consumers are unlikely to trust it when it brings out a new product offering that stretches it into a different area.

Extension traps to avoid

Over the years of working on brand stretch a number of traps have tended to appear repeatedly and are worth bearing in mind when undertaking such an exercise.

The profit cannibalization trap

Some degree of sales cannibalization is inevitable when extending a brand, with the new product stealing some volume from existing products. However, in many cases the problem is made even worse than it needs to be. A couple of years after launch the total business is hardly any bigger than before but is fragmented between more products. The first problem is to propose ideas that are too close to the current product, so encouraging existing brand users to switch. In this case a better route may be to upgrade the core product range.

Secondly, care is not always taken to price the extension so that it is more profitable. In this case, not only does the product cannibalize volume, it reduces the profitability of the total business. Extensions that genuinely offer new benefits can be priced at a premium to dissuade current brand users from switching and also to deliver a better profit margin versus current products. Even if the new launch takes volume from existing products, the profit of the total portfolio will be increased. We saw earlier how Gillette has done this to great effect in the shaving market by launching a number of innovations, each at a higher price and delivering better margins. This boosted operating profit margin from 32.4 per cent in 1987 to 41.2 per cent in 1997, while also growing top-line revenues strongly.

The final way of increasing the risk of cannibalisation is diverting marketing funds for the new launch from the core business. This further weakens the existing business and makes loss of share to competition more likely.

The extra, extra trap

This trap is named after an unsucccesful product range called Extraas that was launched and withdrawn by Häagen Dazs in the 1990s. The idea was to create a new range at a premium price that would be even more indulgent and luxurious than the normal range of Häagen Dazs products. The ingredients were to be especially exotic and the quantities used more generous. However, the pack format was the same and the products did not look that different. The launch diverted effort and money from the main brand and ran the risk of undermining it, as well as confusing consumers. Wasn't Häagen Dazs already about extraordinary indulgence? Did this new range now mean that the old products were no longer as special, or even worse that they weren't that special in the first place? Extraas were really new products that improved on the core propostion and should have been used to refresh and rejuvenate the brand. Indeed, some of the favourite Extraas flavours, such as Caramel Cone Explosion, have now found their rightful place in the Häagen Dazs main brand line-up.

Developing a premium-priced, superior offer can be a successful strategy where the core brand occupies a mainstream positioning and the extension is really different. Nescafé has pulled this off with great results via the launch of its Gold Blend coffee, which now accounts for about one-third of the company's sales in the UK. A combination of new product format and distinctive packaging helped create a genuinely different proposition versus Nescafé Original and justified a premium price. In addition, offering a freeze-dried coffee format rather than powder meant that the product look and feel were different and more expensive. Changing the core brand could have won some users but turned off others, so a better route that allowed more value to be captured was to develop a new sub-branded proposition.

The brand rescue trap

'Rarely does a product alone save a company – the product must reflect a corporate re-positioning or re-focusing', commented marketing journalist Jane Simms accurately (4). However, many teams hope that they can extend themselves out of trouble. A real-life example of this happened with a beer client in Hungary, who was considering the launch of an ice beer under the company's main brand. The brand in question had a solid but rather dull image, offering a well-known and appreciated taste backed by a reputation for brewing excellence built up over many years. I was being briefed on the new product, for which the brand team wanted to develop a positioning and understand its role versus the main brand. I started to smell a rat when I asked how big the new ice beer was likely to be. 'Oh, we expect it to be quite small in volume,' explained the marketing director. 'So why bother launching it?' I enquired. 'The ice beer will have a big impact on the image of the brand and make it more modern and contemporary.' They were hoping it would be what we earlier called an 'image-builder' extension.

Small products tend to be just that, small. They suck valuable money and effort away from the main brand and give back little in return, ending up closer to what we described as 'drains'. As the idea is small, the company finds it hard to invest much money in it, even though the amount of funds spent is likely to be more than its share of sales justifies. The ice beer was unlikely to be so amazing that it would 'punch above its weight' in image terms. Its impact on the brand would be limited and certainly not enough to rescue the whole business. It is true hero products like Apple's iMac, which sold 6 million units in the US during its first two years, that have an impact on brand image. These products are used by many people, creating word of mouth and becoming a highly visible manifestation of the brand promise.

In the case of the beer brand the team was persuaded to reconsider. It decided to focus on developing a pack, product and communication upgrade for the core product, plus looking for other new product ideas with bigger volume potential.

Key takeouts

1 Extensions that are big and bold can build business by attracting new users and creating new usage occasions.

2 Fiddles and tweaks with limited difference to current products risk cannibalizing sales and fragmenting the business. Failing to justify a price premium makes this problem worse by diluting profitability.

3 Extensions by themselves will be unlikely to rejuvenate current products unless the latter are re-invigorated in the spirit of the new launch.

 ## 3-part action plan

Tomorrow

Check to see if your team is in danger of falling into any of the extension traps that we saw earlier. Are there new extensions in the pipeline offering a differentiated proposition at a premium price to deliver incremental sales that are more profitable? Or are they drains that are simply going to eat into existing sales? Are the proposed extensions the best way of delivering the new benefits to the consumer, or are there any that would be better off enhancing and reinforcing the proposition of the core product range?

This month

Start to use the brand and business builder tool as a way of reviewing current and potential new products. Commit to cutting at least 20 per cent of the brand's project list, based on the potential for business and brand building. You and the team will feel liberated and energized by the new focus this will bring and free up valuable time to focus on the projects with best potential.

This year

Over a period of a year you can set the stretchy target of developing one hero product with the potential to be an iMac or a new Beetle. Encourage the team to be more ambitious in its brand stretch work, focusing on the strongest brand in the portfolio and seeing how far it could be extended. Make sure that the market definition it is using is broad enough to give scope for making the footprint of the brand as big as possible.

 **Handover**

We have now seen the different ways in which the brand's external, consumer-facing offer can be used to differentiate versus the competition. The roles of pack, product, communication and extension have all been reviewed. However, there remains one more source of differentiation that demands attention: the people inside the company. We will complete Part IV on Brand action by looking at how to 'Rally the troops'. The next Workout will show how engaging and aligning the internal team can be a powerful source of competitive advantage for both service and product brands.

Workout Eight: Rally the troops

CHAPTER 9

'Men may doubt what you say, but they will believe what you do.'

Lewis Cass

 ## Headlines

Mobilizing the people in the organization behind the brand is key to achieving growth. This requires taking people on a 'journey of commitment' from rational understanding through emotional engagement to alignment of behaviour. However, internal *communication* is only a small part of the answer to this challenge. More important is making big, visible changes in the way the business runs to *dramatize* the vision. Organizational structures and rewards also need to encourage progress towards the vision rather than block progress. Only then can internal communication efforts be used in a supporting and reinforcing role.

People power

A brand-led business can obviously not succeed without strong leadership. No matter how strong the insight, vision and strategy are, without motivating and directing the people in the organization it is impossible to deliver the brand promise consistently. The importance of organizational issues in delivering growth is now fully recognized by marketing directors. In research done by strategic marketing consultancy Added Value on brand growth drivers (1), 'Aligning the organization behind the brand' was rated third with twice the score of 'Advertising in mainstream media' (Table 9.1). Having a brand-supportive organization structure and culture was also rated highly. However, anyone who has suffered rude staff in a coffee bar or poor advice from a helpline knows just how hard it is to get people to be a living, breathing manifestation of the brand. Companies need to move people along a 'journey of commitment', which we will see is a key challenge for both service *and* product companies.

Table 9.1: The drivers of growth (Added Value research with marketing directors, 1999)

Driver		% rating 9 or 10 out of 10
1	Insight into consumer needs	83
2	Clearly defined strategy/positioning	78
3	Brand identity	57
4	Aligning the organization behind the brand	57
5	Training/coaching in best-practice marketing	43
6	Brand-supportive organization structure	41
7	Brand-supportive culture	38
8	Clear measures of brand performance	36
9	Advertising in mainstream media	30
10	Trade partner relations	25

The journey of commitment

To embed a strategy truly within the working fabric of the company, it is necessary to move people along a journey of commitment with three levels (Figure 9.1).

Level 1: Understanding
This level of commitment is based on a rational understanding of the message achieved by informing people of the strategy. People will nod their heads and 'I see your point', agreeing in principle with what has been communicated. However, thinking something is only the first step to making it a reality. It is easy to agree that improving customer satisfaction by being polite and courteous is a good thing; it is something else altogether to do it on a Monday morning when faced with an irate passenger or shopper.

Level 2: Engagement
This higher level of commitment is reached when people have not only been informed of a strategy, they have engaged with it. They feel a more emotional connection with the strategy, feeling inspired and motivated to help make it happen. Engaging people leads to a hard business benefit, as shown in research done by the Hay Group on professional service firms. Offices with 'engaged' employees were as much as 43 per cent more productive, with the five most engaged generating an average of £164 400 in revenue versus £116 100 for the five least (2).

Despite people's best intentions, there may still be important barriers that get in the way. A local marketing director may think and feel that it is best for the company to standardize the packaging and product on a brand that he manages. However, if his boss is

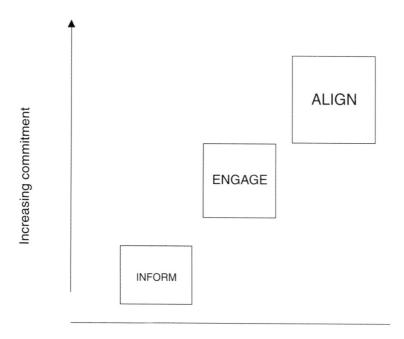

Figure 9.1: The journey of commitment.

measured only on local profit delivery, he will have a hard time pushing through such a move if it is risky for the bottom line.

Level 3: Alignment

The ultimate level of commitment is when behaviours and actions are modified in line with the strategy. This requires not only that people think and feel the right things, the systems, processes and rewards in the business also need to be aligned with the strategy to make change possible. Instead of paying sales people on a commission basis, motor company Daewoo rewarded them based on the percentage of customers who were happy with the experience of buying a car. This was more effective at getting salespeople to stop hard selling and start helping people make the right choice than any number of internal communication events.

Product brands need people too

The need to align and engage the organization behind a brand has always been a concern for service organizations, such as airlines and banks. Here, people in the front line need to be motivated and equipped to deliver the desired service consistently to customers. As we have said, the people are the brand and the brand is the people. However, as business is carried out on a more global scale, winning teams in all companies, including consumer goods businesses, have to move a multitude of stakeholders along the journey of commitment. Motivating the internal audience in a consumer goods business is key to maximizing the share of local marketing budget and effort allocated to your brand versus others in the portfolio. In addition, the success of many major brand strategy projects depends on getting international teams working together to develop and implement growth plans. One of Unilever's biggest challenges in extracting value from the acquisition of Ben & Jerry's and Slimfast will be expanding the brands outside their US home markets. To do this the company will need to engage and align people around the world so that they deliver the brand proposition effectively in their market.

The internal communication trap

More and more companies are using internal communication to try to encourage people to 'live the brand' and move along the journey of commitment. There are even communication agencies specializing in internal marketing to help design and implement such a programme. However, companies now risk falling into the same trap as they did with consumer marketing: outside-in thinking. Time and money are poured into a big song-and-dance show about the brand vision without substantial change being made to the way the business itself is run. You end up with a 'company image wrapper' that is a cosmetic cover-up of problems in the organization. In the same way that consumers are disappointed when a product fails to live up to the promise made in communication, the same goes for employees and the company for which they work. Front-line staff are increasingly feeling 'branded out'.

This problem is illustrated by the framed vision and mission statements that adorn so many plush office receptions. They talk the stuff of consumer service and innovation. However, the people who wrote the words often seem to believe in the saying 'Do as I say, not as I do'. Their own actions and behaviours don't live up to the standards they seek to set for everyone else. One major technology company had as a value 'passion for our people'. Nevertheless, the travel policy meant that people below director level travelled economy class and their bosses were in business class, even when the team travelled together. Before you start urging people in the business team to live the brand, check first that you are taking your own brand medicine.

To make matters worse, many internal communication initiatives start out with good intentions but soon run out of steam. The first issue of an internal brand newsletter tends to arrive with a fanfare and launch party. The second issue follows perhaps a month or two afterwards and then . . . nothing. The project has sailed into the 'Bermuda triangle', never to be seen again, and this understandably breeds cynicism. Any internal communication project should only be started after careful consideration and when there is proper resource in place to keep it going. A way of testing how committed you are is to ask yourself if you are ready to pay an outside company to run it for you; this way you can be sure that the initiative will happen and continue to appear.

In reality, internal communication has a limited role to play in engaging and aligning people with the brand. As the head of internal communication at Vodafone Phil McManus says: 'You don't create a culture, you catch it like a virus. People see new behaviours and copy them until they become "the way we do things round here.".' The place to start, therefore, is with making big, bold changes that dramatize the vision rather than just talking about it. In addition, organizational structures and rewards need to work with the vision, not against it. Only with these fundamental changes in place can internal communication play its full supporting role.

Building commitment

The key to building commitment starts with clear leadership from the top, from what we will call the 'brand CEO'. This can be the CEO of the whole company or a senior director responsible for the brand. The next stage is for the leader to make bold gestures that dramatize the vision; as we saw at the start of the programme, brand actions speak louder than words. Measures and rewards have to be aligned with the new business model and only then should internal communication play a supporting role (Figure 9.2). We will consider each of these four levels in turn.

Leading from the top: The brand CEO

The brand-led business approach works only if the leadership comes from the very top of the organization. We will start by looking at the brand leadership role in mono-branded versus multi-branded businesses.

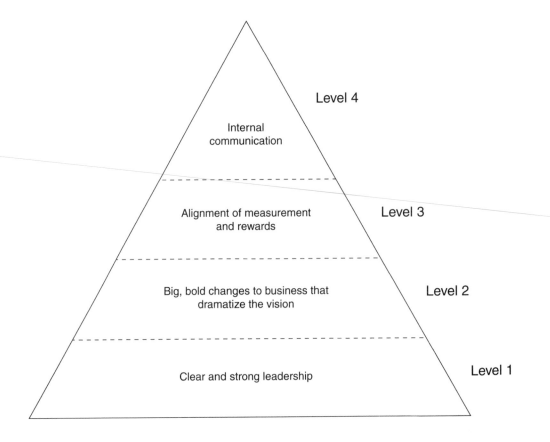

Figure 9.2: Levels of change driving commitment.

Michael, Jeff and the gang

In a mono-branded business such as Dell, Amazon or Starbucks, the company and the brand the consumer buys are one and the same. In many cases the CEO is an inspirational, charismatic leader who is a living, breathing manifestation of the brand. As marketing expert Jack Trout says:

> 'The best leaders know that direction alone is no longer enough. They are in the halls acting as cheerleaders, storytellers and facilitators. They reinforce their sense of direction and vision with words or action' (3).

Indeed, it is hard to separate Bill Gates from Microsoft, Jeff Bezos from Amazon or Michael Dell from Dell. Trout again illustrates this using the example of Herb Kelleher, CEO of the incredibly successful Southwest Airlines: 'The airline's personality is Herb's personality. He is an amazing cheerleader who keeps the planes moving and morale high.'

Learning from effective brand leaders suggests that there are several things that help them mobilize people: believing in the vision, being the brand, writing and telling the brand story and having the power to make change happen.

Believing in the vision

The first and most obvious need is to believe passionately in the vision for the brand itself. If you are not excited and motivated by the purpose, destination and positioning, then there is not a hope in hell that you can get others engaged. If you are lucky, you will have played a leading role in developing the vision and so feel a real sense of ownership and pride. If, on the other hand you have inherited a brand strategy developed by someone else, you may have to work a little harder to achieve the same level of enthusiasm. However, if the vision that has been set is stretchy and challenging, as it should be, the team should only be part of the way towards the destination and your role is to get everyone further down the track. Workout Two, 'Search for true insight', advocated working on a brand that you personally relate to and ideally use yourself. In the same way that this makes generating insights much easier, it helps you to be excited and passionate about the brand vision. You only have to talk to people who work at Egg or Amazon for a few minutes to understand that they are genuinely motivated by what these companies are trying to do. They are passionate about the products and services they market.

Being the brand

The most important thing to do as brand CEO sounds easy but is harder to achieve in practice: be true to the brand values and live them out each day. If you have a value to do with 'innovation and creativity', then you need to be faithful to this in as much of your working life as possible. Do you try to find an interesting and thought-provoking venue for your key business team meetings or merely book the company conference room? Do you use the same old tools and techniques for presenting brand ideas, such as slide presentations on a laptop computer, or do you find new ways of getting the message across that break the mould? For example, one team from a food company conducted a debrief on the results of a project exploring pleasure in cooking by building a kitchen in the office and hiring cooks to demonstrate the findings.

Writing and telling the brand story

Strong brands that engage with people inside the company have a rich and involving story behind them that builds over time. A key part of your role as brand CEO is to be the chief storyteller. Collect and publicly praise examples where people have played an active role in implementing the brand vision. In a service business like a hotel or airline, these could be examples where front-line staff have done a great job of helping solve a consumer problem and received positive feedback. Here is one told by the CEO of the delivery company UPS, Jim Kelly:

> This past December 24, one of our drivers was delivering a package to a military base in Aberdeen, Maryland. It's a busy day for us as you can imagine. The address on one over-night package was incomplete, but rather than drop it off at some base office to be routed to the recipient eventually, she took a lot of extra time to locate the soldier it was intended for. When she did, he was thrilled. It was a surprise gift of airline tickets to bring him home for Christmas – and the plane was leaving in just two hours (4).

For a product-based company it could be an example where a local team has developed a brilliant sales promotion that boosted sales but at the same time also helped communicate the brand positioning. Over time you will start to build up a rich and varied story that will be incredibly helpful as you try to communicate to the team the direction in which you want to take the brand.

Having the power to make change happen

To be a brand CEO and not a brand bureaucrat, you ultimately need to have the power to make things happen. As the CEO this is easy as you are the boss; what Jeff Bezos or Bill Gates says today happens tomorrow. For other, lesser mortals there are two possible solutions. One is that you have a senior sponsor who backs you to the hilt. In Nick Cross's drive to rejuvenate Selfridges, he had the full support of a new Managing Director, Vittorio Radice, who had in turn been hired from Habitat by the CEO of Sears, Liam Strong. The harder route is to assume power and influence, as was the case with David Arkwright in the Top Clean story we saw in the Workout 'Bring your vision to life'. Here, you need to act as if you have the power to make change happen and be incredibly persuasive in engaging people to join your mission.

Multi-brand companies

In multi-brand companies such as Unilever or Procter & Gamble, the concept of brand leadership is also evolving. With a more focused portfolio, the biggest brands are global, billion-dollar businesses in their own right and global brand directors are being appointed to run them. The risk is that these directors end up as toothless coordinators, fighting an

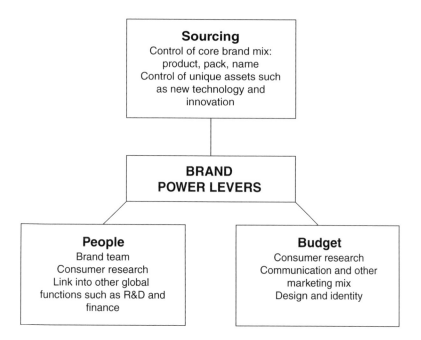

Figure 9.3: Key sources of power in global brand management.

up-hill battle with local general managers to produce synergies, share best practice and drive out costs. To truly add value they need to play the role of the global brand CEO and in order to do this they need control of *people*, *money* and *sourcing* (Figure 9.3). A bigger team means more human capital that can be mobilized to run projects and get things done. More money means bigger budgets for research, innovation and brand mix development. Control over sourcing means that only you decide the product design, formula and packaging. These changes will mean less power for local general managers, but only in this way is there a hope of running a truly brand-led business on a global scale.

When appointing and managing brand CEOs, a problem to address is the 'new broom syndrome', where marketing people spend only 12–18 months before moving to a new assignment. These frequent changes in brand leadership cause constant shifts in strategy, as each new person takes a different approach to 'make their mark'. This causes confusion for the consumer and is a huge waste of organizational energy and money. Each change in strategy eats up time and budget as the whole business goes through a new learning curve. However, when the turnover of brands is measured in billions rather than millions, senior management is starting to recognize the need for more continuity in leadership teams.

The local/global interface

Balancing the need for global coherence and local relevance remains one of the toughest challenges for any brand-led business. First-hand experience with leading companies such as Unilever, P&G, Disney and Mars shows that no one has yet found the perfect solution. One firm conclusion is that companies need to be clearer and more transparent about how the organization has to work and make the tough decisions required to remove ambiguity, duplication and confusion. The two main options that seem to be available are truly global and multi-local.

Truly global

In this kind of organization the drive towards global branding is pushed through to its endpoint: 'Think global, act global' is the mantra here. This is the model pursued by P&G, Gillette and Amazon. A central, global team controls all the three key levers of sourcing, people and budget. Packaging, product, design, naming and communication are completely harmonized to achieve maximum cost savings. A Gillette advert in the UK might have a different voiceover and actor from that in the US, but that's about the extent of the differences. This also allows rapid roll-out of new innovations and upgrades. Local and even regional marketing teams are cut back to the minimum and only work on promotions, PR and other activities that have to be done at a national level.

This approach works well in a company like P&G that has always had a rather military, 'command-and-control' culture where local teams are used to accepting orders from HQ. Key brands such as Pampers and Always have also been globally harmonized from the start. A readiness to push through painful organizational change is required, as local teams need to be dramatically downsized.

The downside is that there are fewer opportunities for reacting to local consumer needs and competitive threats. However, companies like P&G believe that this is more than offset by the benefits of global harmonization.

Multi-local

This approach requires more of a balance to be found between local and global priorities. The balancing act is extremely hard and makes this kind of organization harder to run in many ways than the truly global one. Unilever, Kellogg's and Danone are examples of companies trying to do this. They have a history of promoting local autonomy and have senior teams of people in place in key markets. There tend also to be major differences in brand name, design, formulation and communication.

Global teams are put in place and need to work in a 'matrix' structure where local teams report in to them *and* the country or regional general manager. The central team is tasked with defining a global brand vision, positioning and core mix with the input of regional and local teams. Countries are then tasked with 'activating' the brand through promotions, events and PR, but also have the possibility of doing some local innovation and communication. People, budget and sourcing are shared between global and local teams with the latter often having the balance of power.

This web can easily become a nightmare to navigate through, especially when rewards and recognition are not aligned. The classic example we have already seen is when local management is measured only on profit, so that it pays little or no attention to requests to be a 'good global citizen' if this hurts the bottom line. Attempts to harmonize the brand are strongly resisted as this means giving up control of sourcing and so having power taken away. The central team often ends up playing the role of a brand bureaucrat, not a brand CEO.

To have a chance of being effective the company needs to get off the fence and accept that the priority is a global brand, with local sensitivity important but secondary. Two main changes then have to be made to reflect this. First, the global team should have increased control of the core brand mix, especially product, pack, design and name where management must be 'tight'. It is here that the most important economies of scale are to be found. Also, harmonization of these components makes innovation much easier and faster. An initial step is to harmonize positioning, design and product while keeping local names, as Unilever has done with its 'teddy bear' brand of fabric softeners, called Cajoline in France and Snuggle in the US. On other areas such as brand activation the management can be more 'loose', allowing greater local freedom. Even advertising development, often the most high profile of mix elements in discussions on harmonization, seems to be much less important than manufacturing and purchasing in terms of generating economies. This is shown in the results of Added Value's research into growth drivers with marketing directors (Table 9.2). If one big factory is producing a single product for Europe, as with Pampers (count the number of languages on the pack, there are about 10), then you can afford to let two or three key markets shoot their own films. It is also standardization of product and packaging that allows faster roll-out of innovation.

Secondly, measurement and rewards should be aligned with the global objective. We will review this issue later in more detail, but the main aspects are to review local managers on business results and their contribution to the global vision. Young managers in many companies still feel that they need to 'do their own thing' to get promoted. In contrast, at P&G the emphasis is on business results, with young managers being actively encouraged

Table 9.2: Savings and benefits of global harmonization (Added Value research with marketing directors, 1999)

	% top 2 boxes (9 + 10)
Purchasing	51%
Manufacturing	51%
Quicker international roll-out of innovation	39%
Research and development	32%
Advertising production	17%
Opportunity for global/international marketing support	15%
Sales force and distribution	13%
Media buying	12%
Packaging design development	7%
Marketing team overhead	6%
Average	24%

to 'steal with pride' from other markets with a successful mix. This culture makes it easier for ideas to spread through the 'success virus', where ideas are developed locally and then the best are picked up by other markets. Many great successes, such as Timotei shampoo, McDonald's McFlurry ice cream and Studio Line hair-styling products, have become global brands in this way. To encourage the spread of the success virus, both the 'transmitters' and the 'receivers' need to be recognized and rewarded for their efforts.

 ## 5-minute workout

Are you walking the talk when it comes to living out the vision for the brand? Write down the four to five key things you are asking of people in the business to bring the vision to life for consumers. Rate yourself out of ten based on how faithfully you apply the same principles in the way you do your job on a day-to-day basis.

Having a brand CEO to lead the way is the first step in engaging and aligning people to deliver the brand promise. However, they will struggle by themselves to communicate the brand's vision and positioning effectively to everyone. We will now go on to look at how teams can work with the brand leader to engage and align the whole organization.

Do as I do, not as I say

The best way to communicate the desired vision for a brand is to change the brand itself. Nick Cross, Chief Marketing Officer of Egg, talks about making 'big, bold changes' accompanied by a 'sound bite' that sums up the new direction. When he was marketing director at Selfridges, the changes made to the shop windows were as much to show people in the store the new direction as they were to signal change to shoppers. The sound bite of 'The spirit of the city' captured the energy, innovation and youthfulness that the team wanted to inject into the store. To engage people with the brand vision the whole brand mix can be used, including communication, product and people.

Communication

Good brand communication can do more than pages of presentation to bring the brand to life in a memorable and involving way. Apple's 'Think different' television campaign run at the end of the 1990s celebrated original thinkers and doers such as Einstein and Muhammad Ali. It was a rousing anthem that communicated the renaissance of Apple following the return of Steve Jobs. This advertising did a job for the brand with consumers, but also made people proud of working for Apple and reminded them about the brand's values and vision.

At a more basic level, many brand teams fail to achieve effective communication internally about what the brand is doing in its consumer marketing plan. People working for the brand discover the advertising when sitting at home watching television like any other viewer. In contrast to this, Vodafone employees received postcards depicting the new television campaign with their payslip. These said when the new adverts would break and on what channel, building anticipation and involvement.

Even worse than not keeping people informed is when the advertising alienates rather than engages employees. One wonders whether IKEA staff were that impressed by recent advertising that portrayed them owning up to awful service and justifying this by the low prices. When working with an Internet retailer I was questioned by a confused member of the business team: 'You're a clever consultant, can you explain what our advertising is supposed to mean?' How can you expect people in the business to 'live the brand' when they don't even relate to or understand its advertising?

The opposite extreme of these examples is the Halifax bank in the UK, which has gone as far as making its staff the stars of its commercials. Real bank employees like Howard do song-and-dance numbers promoting products on TV and they are even named at the end of the spots (Figure 9.4). The commercials have struck a chord with viewers and there has been a sharp rise in brand awareness. At the same time, it is no surprise that people working for the bank are incredibly positive about the exercise. It celebrates their contribution to the success of the business and gives them the chance of 30 seconds of fame, a big motivation given people's fascination with 'reality TV'.

Figure 9.4: Halifax communication.

Reproduced by permission of Halifax plc.

Hero products

A step better than even the marketing mix is the creation of hero products. More than any other tool or technique, products can bring to life the brand idea in a visible and enduring fashion. The iMac was a breathtaking dramatization of Apple's re-discovered talent for designing user-friendly, great-looking computers. Most importantly, it flew off the shelves, helping get the company back to growth and saving it from the risk of bankruptcy or a hostile takeover. It also served to inspire and guide the design team better than any brand statement, strategy or book could have done. A range of mould-breaking and image-building products have followed, such as the iBook, G4 Titanium Powerbook and now the iPod MP3 player. The new Beetle for Volkswagen and the Mach 3 razor from Gillette are other examples of brilliant new products that have boosted sales and brand image but also inspired and guided the whole organization.

People

As Professor Manfred Kets de Vries at INSEAD once told me, 'The only person that likes change is a wet baby.' Not everyone will be able to embrace the new vision for a brand and business. In too many cases, leaders take what seems to be the easy way out and leave these people in place. However, in the long run this policy backfires by allowing 'brand vandals' to stay in the organization, preventing the rest of the team from working towards the vision. During the re-launch of Selfridges, the polyester uniforms that staff wore were discarded and instead they were asked to make their own choice of clothes in tune with the brands they were selling. Most of the people working in the store saw this as liberating and enjoyed dressing in a way that fitted with Boss, Gucci or Paul Smith. For the first time, young girls turned up in t-shirts that revealed their midriff and belly button piercing. This shocked some of the old guard on the board, but was much closer to the way that prospective customers were dressing. In contrast, other employees felt exposed without their uniform to hide behind and made no effort to dress for success; they saw the change as a hindrance, not a liberation. Rather than letting these people stay on, they were let go. This avoided the problem of brand vandalism and let the rest of the team get on with the job of building the business in line with the new vision.

At a more basic level, many service organizations are unrealistic about the level of brand engagement they can expect from staff on the front line who are often poorly paid and have limited prospects. Most of us if we were paid £5 an hour to wait on tables or run a video shop would do the minimum needed to get the job done and try to have a few laughs on the

Table 9.3: Team member benefits at Prêt à Manger

- Pay of at least £5.25 per hour with average £6.75
- 'Great night out' for teams who excel
- Holiday pay from day 1
- Earn sick leave through good performance
- Early start but also early finish
- Twice-yearly company party
- Chances of development: 60% of managers started as team members
- Unpaid sabbaticals
- £20 for maternity jeans, 10 weeks' full pay and childcare vouchers for new mums
- Up to £2000 paid for introducing new staff

way to relieve the boredom. Living the brand would not be high on our agenda. In contrast, successful companies like Starbucks and Prêt à Manger do offer benefits and development opportunities that give employees a little more incentive to try harder to deliver against the brand promise (Table 9.3).

What gets measured, gets done

'What gets measured, gets done' were the words of wisdom of one general manager at P&G. He understood just how important the alignment of performance measurement was in helping to deliver the organization's strategic priorities. The drive for a brand-led business approach can be scuppered by a failure to align rewards and recognition in line with the strategy. People at all levels must be incentivized to support the brand vision actively if it is to have a chance of becoming reality. For example, I worked with Walt Disney's European Vice President who was valiantly striving to get local companies to do promotions that fitted better with Disney's image. He had quantitative data showing a risk to the brand from overexposure and the 'slapping' of Disney characters on everything from batteries to toilet rolls. However, local managers were rewarded on the financial level of deals they made, with no recognition of their impact on brand equity enhancement or destruction. The brand director was trying to push water up a very steep hill and made little progress.

The concept of the 'balanced scorecard' is now being used by many companies. This transparent and widely shared 'dashboard' of performance measures helps everyone know if the brand and business objectives are being achieved. These measures give a clear indication of what the leaders of the business consider to be important aspects of performance. In the case of Frito-Lay, the snacks and drinks business, five main headings have been used covering 'brand', 'consumer', 'customer', 'product' and 'financial'. These different measures work together to encourage a brand-led business approach, as they require financial results at the same time as building brand equity and product quality (Figure 9.5). These measures can also be 'cascaded' down the different levels of the organization in a connected fashion. Everyone in the business understands what they are being measured on and how this contributes to the achievement of the higher-order goals. As Carol Welch, Global Brand Director at Cadbury Schweppes, remembers from her days at Frito-Lay:

> Every month you had to report against the key performance indicators, and you knew that if you were below objective on any of them you better have a very good explanation, and a plan to fix it.

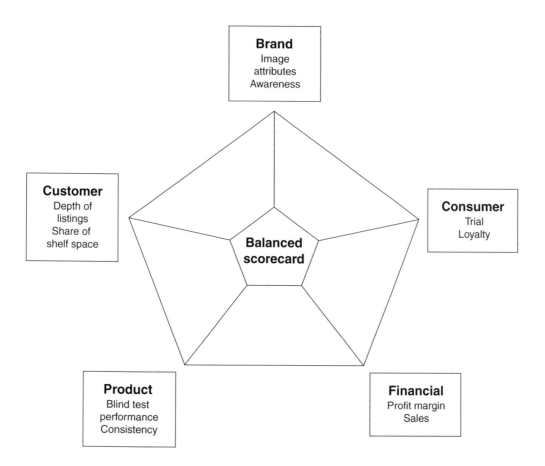

Figure 9.5: Example of balanced scorecard from Frito-Lay.

Once this method of working becomes embedded in a company it turns into an incredibly potent form of everyday self-regulation. People refer back to the measures for clarification of the best way forward. One consultant explained how at Tesco the people he talked to on projects were always referring to the 'steering wheel', which is their balanced scorecard measurement system.

The power of measurement to guide the organization's efforts can be seen at Amazon, which has the benefit of a young organization that is supple and relatively easy to mould. Each function is headed up by a senior global manager who sets the performance standards for his or her area, such as the cost of acquiring a new customer in the case of marketing. These targets are what drive the efforts of local functional heads. In their strive to improve efficiency and effectiveness, they can only hit the benchmarks by cooperating with other functions. So marketing must liaise with customer service to check support centre staffing when starting a heavy advertising campaign. Otherwise they run the risk of frustrating and losing new customers who cannot get the help they need. In this performance-driven organization there is a limited need to force functional heads to talk to one another and collaborate, as they *have* to do this in order to hit their targets. This means that the requirement for general management at a local level is much less than in a traditional company. This role is increasingly played by a junior project manager, with the most senior and highest-performing people playing the functional roles. This allows people to focus on building functional excellence while still providing people who have genuine general management ability with opportunities for a limited number of truly important jobs that need this skill, such as regional presidents.

The supporting role of internal communication

Provided that the bedrock of business change is in place, with measures and rewards aligned, internal communication can support in moving people along the journey of commitment. The basic rule for internal communication is to make it as simple and practical as possible. It should be rooted in the reality of life on the front line and avoid the dry theory and empty war cries of many corporate presentations. For example, a team in one retail business created a mini-soap opera set in a typical store, literally to dramatize the difference between good and bad service. This was much more successful at engaging people than a classic set of slides would have been. We will look in more detail below at the role that can be played by brand books, brand television and brand events.

Brand books

Brand books started life as design guides, used by companies to lay down specific rules on how the brand identity should be applied, but over time they have evolved to cover much more. The history of the brand is often given, providing useful background information that is especially important where heritage is a key part of the brand positioning. The brand strategy is explained in some detail to help teams understand where the brand is trying to head and the sort of marketing mix that should be developed. Some brand books go as far as to have a communication kit that provides visuals and creative elements that can be used by local marketing teams to develop promotional or advertising materials. This has the benefits of saving time for local teams and also ensuring a consistency of executional style.

The risk with brand books is that they end up being bulky, boring reference books that do no more than gather dust on the shelf. Again, shortcuts in production mean that many of them are presented in standard lever-arch files and look like a set of rigid guidelines and rules to be applied at all times. In contrast, the brand guidelines produced by Egg's brand communication team were a million miles away from this traditional approach. The team used a large-format magazine written in a chatty and informal style to get across the brand idea. Much use was made of 'Egg is' and 'Egg isn't' examples photos and even customer letters, to illustrate the right tone and feel for brand communication. The magazine format meant that the guidelines could easily be carried around in a briefcase rather than having to be stacked on a shelf.

Brand television

The next level of internal brand communication makes use of sound and moving images to bring to life the brand idea you have created, as done by the Lynx/Axe global brand team and its advertising agency BBH. Their two-minute video is all you would need to brief anyone on the brand, whether a new hire, creative agency or local brand team. The video communicates key positioning elements such as target audience, consumer insight and brand personality, but does this in a highly entertaining and memorable way with a cheeky tone and style that are absolutely on brand. A naked male model uses boards containing the words of the strategy to cover his private parts. He reveals the boards one at a time until they are all gone, accompanied by a Monty Pythonesque voiceover.

Brand events

No matter how good the brand book or video, the ultimate form of internal brand communication is of course face to face and live, although this is also the most expensive and time consuming to organize. Also, the live event runs the huge risk of falling into the 'statue-revealing' trap, where energy levels are high on the day only to fall back to normal levels afterwards.

One-off events are typically used to mark an important milestone, such as the re-launch of a brand, a new product introduction or, increasingly, a new team created as a result of a merger. The most basic principle is to use an interactive, two-way process and not just a 'show-and-tell' event, where senior management explains the strategy and what is expected of everybody. When two food companies were brought together for the first time after a merger, rather than merely talking to the audience the team running the event involved them. Teams of people were put together and had to cook a typical dish of a particular country that was not their own, with the results of their work being eaten by the group that night as dinner. This exercise resulted in people from both companies working together and so getting to know each other. It did this in a way that was fun and also linked to the mission of the business, rather than having them out in the cold doing an outward bound course. The event was one of the most memorable parts of the conference and people in the business still talk about it today, more than a year later.

Cascade programmes are a more sophisticated form of internal communication. They have the benefit of reaching a much larger audience than a one-off event, at the same time as letting people work in small teams on practical applications of the strategy. A group of 'champions' or 'ambassadors' is created from people who are good communicators and enthusiastic supporters of the new strategy. They are then taken through an intensive programme so that they understand the communication task. A kit of materials is provided to help them run a number of programmes in the business with front-line staff. The kit contains materials such as brand videos and books plus interactive exercises to bring the strategy to life and work on personal action planning. A huge cascade process has been used by one global technology company to communicate the new vision for the business to all several hundred thousand staff (Figure 9.6).

Too often, a cascade programme is treated as a single exercise that inevitably has limited or no impact on the business. It is quickly forgotten and people wait for the next exercise to be carried out in a year or two's time. Another problem is that the quality of the cascade can be variable in quality and even in completion, with some ambassadors half-hearted in their follow-up. To be effective, a cascade programme must be integrated into the development

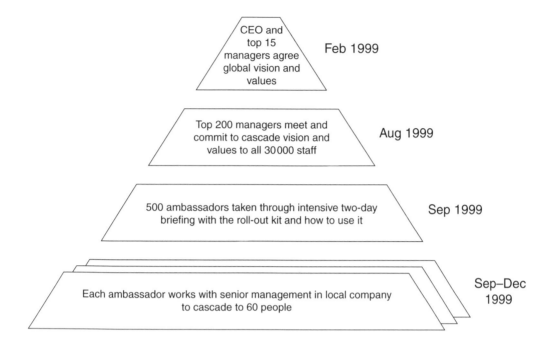

Figure 9.6: Example of cascade programme.

and reward systems already in place. Feedback on the quality of the ambassador's cascade events should be requested from front-line staff and included in performance reviews. In the same way, the personal action plans should be integrated into the work plan and coaching of front-line staff, with their line managers informed and involved in this process. Also, any cascade programme should be treated as a minimum two- to three-year process, with several waves of activity that build over time. Only with this sustained effort does such a project have any chance of moving people through the commitment journey.

Measuring effectiveness

As with everything else we have covered so far, measuring the effectiveness of internal communication should be handled with the same thoroughness and professionalism as that of external communication. However, many internal brand communication programmes have no or limited research put in place to evaluate success, despite the large sums of money involved in carrying them out. The most important thing to bear in mind is to ensure that there is a 'pre' measure among the target audience to obtain a baseline reading on the key questions. These questions should cover a range of issues that span thinking, feeling and doing. Some examples are below:

- *Thinking*: How well do you understand the brand's strategy? How clear is the role you need to play in delivering the vision?
- *Feeling*: How involved do you feel in helping achieve the objectives set out for the brand? How excited are you by the new vision?
- *Doing*: How much have you changed the way you do your day-to-day job to reflect the brand vision? How seriously do you think people around you take the new strategy? How important in your personnel and salary review is your delivery of the vision?

The other key consideration is to have waves of research that tie into the internal marketing efforts. While it is important to get a reading just after key events, it is also necessary to track how things change over time.

Key takeouts

1 Brand leadership must come from the top. Without strong direction and motivation from the brand CEO, internal communication efforts will flounder.
2 Brand actions speak much louder than words. Focus on changing the brand itself, the measurement and the rewards to avoid the risk of internal communication creating an image wrapper that covers up underlying problems.
3 Internal communication should be practical, true to life and engaging to have the best chance of success.

 ## 3-part action plan

Tomorrow

Conduct a quick review of the internal communication initiatives that are currently underway, bearing in mind the traps we have seen. Are they reinforcing and supporting real change in the brand and business or merely serving as an image wrapper? Are there plans in place to ensure follow-through and sustaining efforts, or is there a risk that you will run a one-off, 'big bang' event that creates short-term impact but no long-term benefit? When you review your product development pipeline, do you see anything that could be as powerful as the iMac in manifesting the brand's positioning, or are all they all run-of-the-mill ideas?

This month

Review the measurement systems in place and assess how effective they are in helping people run a brand-led business. Is there a balanced scorecard that is visible to the whole team and helps guide their actions and are the top-line measures cascaded down to a team and individual level? If not, how can you influence the setting up of such a system?

This year

Work on the brand mix to ensure that it is serving as a dramatic manifestation of the brand vision. Keep in mind the internal audience when developing brand communication: how effective is it as a rallying call for the team? In terms of people, try to ensure that you have weeded out the brand vandals and that rewards and prospects are sufficient to achieve the level of performance you aspire to.

 Handover

We have now come to the end of the eight *Brand Gym* Workouts. This programme should help you move from brand foundations, through to brand strategy and on to brand action. We have looked at the role of the external mix and the people inside the business. The final part of the book will suggest ways of building 'Brand stamina', with a chapter to help you 'Stay in shape, keep the faith'. This will propose ways of ensuring that training and coaching are effective at helping you learn and apply the principles of brand-led business.

Part V

BRAND STAMINA

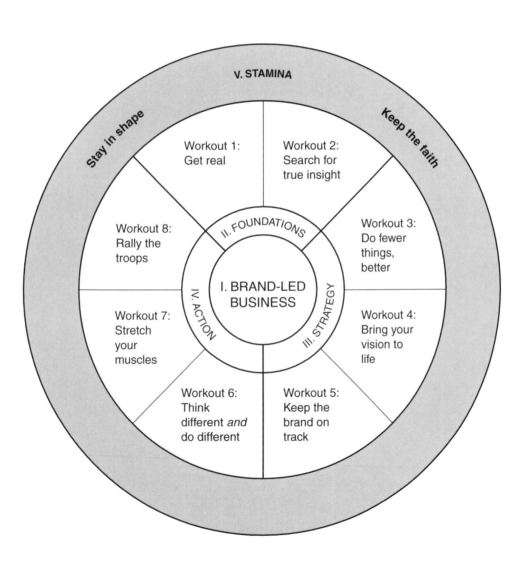

Stay in shape, keep the faith

'A good resolution is like an old horse which is often saddled and never ridden.'

Mexican proverb

 Headlines

Sticking to any exercise programme is hard; it's all too easy to slip back into the old routine and lose the good habits you set out determined to keep. This applies to sporting endeavours but also to the world of business. Having a clear idea of the areas you need to improve on and a clear exercise programme to address these needs will help you stay on top of your game. Where possible, coaching on the models and principles of 'brand think' should be done by discussing the practical, real-life issues of 'brand do'.

Research by Esporta fitness clubs found that 70 per cent of people drop out of their club after six months. The company has invested in programmes to support members and help them keep up their motivation. The same challenge of staying in shape exists in the sphere of brands and business, as described by one senior director in an international food business:

> It's all too easy to forget the good principles of strategy and positioning, especially when you are under time pressure. You can end up buying a piece of advertising because it feels comfortable and familiar, even though it might not be right for the long-term future of the brand.

This last chapter is designed to give you some practical tips and tricks to help you apply the principles of brand-led business on a day-to-day basis (Table 10.1).

Fitness check

Before starting any physical exercise programme you assess your fitness, and the same should be true with brand-led business. A thorough audit of strengths and weaknesses

Table 10.1: Recap of Workouts and the problems they solve

Workout	Problem	Solution
1 Get real	Strategy is too theoretical	Ensure that strategy drives action
2 Search for true insight	Expensive consumer research that stifles innovation	Use insight to illuminate and inform, not as a crutch
3 Do fewer things, better	Fragmentation of resources across too many brands	Focus on fewer brands to boost return on investment
4 Bring your vision to life	Vision as a generic statement framed on the wall	Create an ambitious, inspiring vision
5 Keep the brand on track	Brand positioning as theoretical box filling	Positioning to drive a competitive and coherent brand mix
6 Think different *and* do different	Lacking the courage truly to differentiate the brand	Be brave enough to create a disruptive mix
7 Stretch your brand muscles	Small brand extension 'fiddles' that fragment brand	Launch big, bold extensions to create growth
8 Rally the troops	Reliance on internal communication to create change	Dramatize the vision with real action and align rewards

can be carried out at both a group and individual level, using the eight Workouts and associated human qualities from this programme, or using another list of criteria that you can develop (Figure 10.1). Criteria should be weighted in importance, to distinguish 'make-or-break' criteria from those that are just 'nice to have'. Each criteria can then be scored to get an idea of the team's performance profile. The results of this audit should help guide and inspire the development of an exercise plan for the year to develop strengths and address weaknesses.

If you are training for a marathon you cannot succeed without clear measures of your progress, so each week you record the miles run in each session and the time taken. Your exercise schedule is designed to build up your endurance over time and it is easy to track how well you are doing against your target. In the same way, you will need to get clear measures of how you and your team are progressing towards your objectives. Some of this feedback should be objective data such as brand equity measures, share results and profitability. Other measures can be more qualitative, with the team rating its members on key criteria at the year, half-way through and again at the end.

Exercise programme

Sports teams have a sophisticated exercise programme to help them achieve their performance objectives, with varying levels of intensity. A typical week will have a combination of team practice, video analysis of last week's game, weight training in the gym and

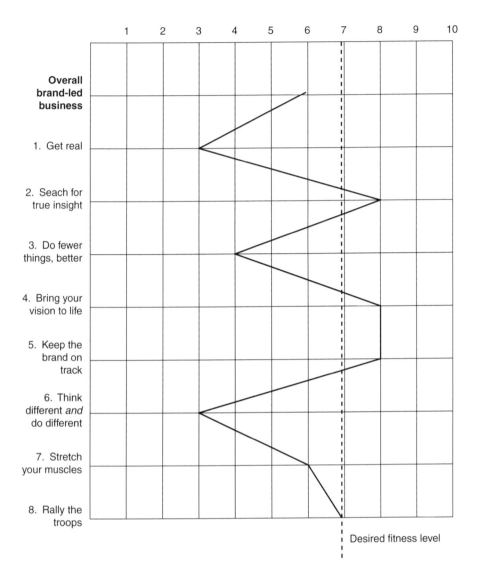

Figure 10.1: Fitness check.

conditioning from the team physio. The level of energy and conditioning is designed to peak for the big game at the weekend and across a season there is also a pattern of activity, with the need to get off to a good start but then re-adjust and re-plan based on early results to keep the team on track. Over a year, top athletes spend about 5–10 per cent of their time in high-performance mode and the rest getting and staying in shape.

In contrast to their sporting counterparts, brand teams are expected to be at peak performance permanently; it seems like every day is match day in the business world, with its non-stop series of briefings, meetings and projects. Training, coaching and conditioning are sporadic and infrequent, with most managers lucky to get a few days off a year to refresh, reflect and work on their intellectual muscles and stamina. The more senior you are, the less time you tend to have to recharge the mental batteries, even though you need to do this more, if anything. However, to have a chance of improving your performance and not just doing business as usual, you will need to re-engineer your work programme to free up space for 'working out' on the areas highlighted in your fitness assessment.

One global brand team in a major consumer goods company set out to do just this, deciding to free up a few hours of each of their four key meetings across the year to spend this on improving performance in a key area of brand-led business. The global brand director designed these sessions based on feedback from the team members on how they saw their fitness against each of the eight *Brand Gym* Workouts. For example, in one session the team focused on the 'Get real' Workout, as they were concerned that too much of the strategic work they had been developing was theoretical and not tied clearly enough to business-building activities. In another they worked at 'Stretch your muscles' to be sure that the proposed brand extensions were performing well on both the brand- and business-building dimensions.

Using brand do to learn brand think

When developing a brand exercise programme, efforts should be made to avoid the traditional focus on the theory of brands and marketing, in the hope that people will then apply what they have learnt back on the job. As we all know from our own experience, 90 per cent or more of what goes into our heads on most courses is forgotten quickly and never used. Training manuals sit in the cupboard collecting dust and we go back to our old ways of working. For a while I was a tutor on the brand management training programme for one of the world's biggest and best consumer goods companies, putting over 100 managers through their paces. We looked at the theory of brand think and tried to use case studies to bring it to life, using famous examples such as Nike, Volvo and Coca-Cola. But no matter how hard we tried, there was still a big disconnect between the world of the training course and life in the trenches back on the job.

At Starbucks and other great brand-led businesses in the service sector, the use of training is different. A great deal of time and money is spent at store level to train people on what it takes to deliver the Starbucks experience. Detailed attention is paid to coffee preparation, store ambience and greeting customers. This combination of little details makes up the brand concept and so being trained to deliver them consistently is being trained to deliver the brand promise; the brand is the business is the brand. As people are being trained to do their day-to-day job, they retain more of what they have learnt. They apply the key principles immediately and in doing so learn about the brand promise and how to play an active role in delivering against it. In other words, they are using brand do to learn about brand think.

Perhaps other companies could be inspired by Starbucks' example to change the way they use training radically. In the case of a consumer goods company, you could train all the people who work on the same brand together, rather than all the people from the same region. For example, 20 or so brand managers working on Dove could come together to learn about the brand vision, positioning and strategy (brand think). At the same time they could work on how this is applied in the business on advertising, packaging and promotions (brand do). As with Starbucks, by making the training directly linked to people's job, the chances of remembering the learning are improved. The course could be designed to ensure that people were also building their mastery of the portable tools and techniques needed to work on other brands. However, rather than the tools and techniques being the way into the learning, they get 'smuggled' into the programme by being used to work on ways of building the brand and business.

Get a coach

Even the best athletes in the world at the peak of their sport benefit from coaching. Michael Schumacher, Tiger Woods and David Beckham are all seeking to raise their game and would struggle to do this by themselves, no matter how driven they are. A coach can take an independent view of the athlete's capabilities and potential, informed by having seen many other cases before. They can push and encourage the sports person to take their performance to new levels. The coach can bring new techniques, exercises and tools to help enable progress to be made, refreshing the exercise regime to make it more effective and more productive. And when times are tough and morale low, it can help to have someone to remind you of what you are fighting for and what can be achieved with the right effort. It's easier to stick to a training programme if you know someone is waiting for you in the gym at a set time.

So why shouldn't brand teams also make use of a coach to help them raise their game, stay in shape and keep the faith? One barrier to this is money, but many senior managers find funds to pay for expensive consultants, sometimes an army of them, to help answer difficult problems. Nevertheless, when used *too* often this becomes like hiring a chauffeur to drive your car for you. If you delegate too much responsibility you can become lazy and also miss out on the enjoyment that driving can provide. An alternative approach is to spend some of this budget on getting a brand coach to help you and the team work through the problem for yourself. From experience, this more collaborative approach is cheaper, makes more use of the talent you have and creates a greater sense of ownership for the solution.

Another objection is that the marketing director should be the coach and play this role for the team and this can be a good solution in an ideal world. Of course, he or she should be playing a coaching role on a day-to-day basis on key projects. However, how many of these senior people have time really to stay up to speed with the latest tools and techniques and to learn from the practices of other companies outside their field? Some may have this opportunity, but many are just too busy and so could benefit from a little outside support to help them. And how easy will they find it to have a neutral, external perspective on the issues?

A word of caution is required on exactly what is meant by coaching in the context of marketing and brand teams. Coaching can help a team in two main areas: the 'What?' and the 'How?' of doing business. The first of these tackles specific problems such as how to re-position a brand or how to organize the brand architecture. The second question is more to do with the way a team works together, in terms of roles, behaviours and process. Team building has become fairly popular in many companies, who spend a fortune sending people into the jungle or making them abseil down high buildings. The positive impact of these sorts of exercises on brand and business team performance is yet to be proved. Members of a sports team have to support each other physically in high-pressure situations, even if this means suffering pain, so you can see the benefit of putting them into testing environments that seek to replicate the same conditions off the field. However, it is less obvious that putting people through hell and high water pays off when the challenge they need to face lasts months rather than 90 minutes and when the exercise is more intellectual than physical.

A better approach is to tackle the 'How?' at the same time as the 'What?' by working together on a real problem. For example, a team lacking a shared sense of purpose may also not work well together, with everyone trying to hog the airtime and not listening to the others. A coach could help the team work together to develop a brand purpose, using some new techniques and exercises to get the task done in a more productive and enjoyable fashion.

Key takeouts

1 Business people, like athletes, need an exercise programme to stay in shape.
2 Most training separates brand think from brand do, leading to a large amount of 'learning leakage'. Linking these two elements more closely will increase effectiveness.

3 Be cautious about working on the 'How?' of teamwork in isolation. Work on specific issues to do with the 'What?' of brand building as a way of learning new ways of working together.

 ## 3-part action plan

Tomorrow

Take a long, hard look at the team and organization in which you are working and ask yourself how well it is designed to help you stay in shape and keep the faith. Do you have in place the basic elements of a clear vision, an exercise programme and a way of measuring progress? When was the last time you and your team had some coaching that genuinely helped you work more effectively on building the brand and business?

This month

Work with the team to carry out an audit of your capabilities and performance levels to assess areas of strength and opportunities for improvement. Using the two questions of 'What?' and 'How?' highlight areas on which you need to work during the coming year. Then develop ideas on what the right exercise regime would be to help you raise your game. What new skills or abilities do you need to learn? Would you benefit from bringing in a brand coach to help inspire, guide and challenge you to raise your game? And do you have across the months some variation in type and level of activity, including at least a few periods of recuperation, stimulation and refreshment?

This year

Over the year you should be able to make a genuine impact at a personal, team and organizational level to ensure that people stay in shape and keep the faith. You can take responsibility for ensuring that the team's exercise programme is implemented and not sacrificed at the altar of other meetings and business commitments. Ensure that the objectives are integrated with the personal development plans and performance reviews of the people concerned. When designing training try to use brand do to learn about brand think, rather than focusing on the theory of brands and marketing.

Handover

We have now come to the end of *The Brand Gym* programme. I hope that the eight Workouts have provided you with some practical, real-world ideas on how to boost your brand and business performance. With a little luck you may even have started to put into practice some of the 5-minute workouts or 3-part action plans. Don't forget, people count more than process, so the best place to start may well be the audit described in this last chapter. Good luck!

Air-raid shelter syndrome: putting every idea possible into a positioning and so ending up with a strategy that is flabby and unfocused. Often a sign of 'strategy by committee'.

Brand (true): a name and symbols associated with a known and trusted customer experience that appeals to the head and heart.

Brand bureaucracy: artificial separation of 'brand think' (strategy) and 'brand do' (implementation). Leads to wasting time and money on theoretical and academic strategic posturing.

Brand-led business: Leading the organization to deliver consistently against the promise of a motivating and differentiated customer experience.

Brand portfolio strategy: balancing 'how many brands you need' against 'how many brands you can feed'.

Brand static: advertising that shouts at the top of its voice without anything interesting to say.

Brand wannabes: products dressed up in brand clothing but lacking the power to be brands in a true sense.

Consumer empathy: a deeper, more visceral level of insight that comes from being the consumer or at least having a genuine passion for the category.

Innokill: premature use of quantitative screening to filter out new ideas that may be radical and unconventional.

Journey of commitment: moving people in the organization from rational understanding to emotional engagement through to alignment of behaviour.

Megabrand: combine the 3 Ss of business scale, geographic scope and product stretch.

Navel gazing: getting so close to their brand that you overestimate the importance of many of the small issues on which you are working.

Outside-in branding: approach to brands that focuses on the exterior look and feel ('image wrapper') rather than the totality of the product or service.

Polishing the pyramid: perfecting the strategy and testing it to death before using it to brief mix development.

Undercover research: using 'covert' techniques such as immersion and decoding to generate deeper and richer insights.

Working in a vacuum: seeing strategy as a theoretical exercise that has a value in its own right, rather than as a means to the end of profitable growth.

References

Chapter 1

1 Times Online, 12 February 2002.
2 Malmsten, E., Portanger, E. and Drazin, C. (2001) *Boo Hoo*, Random House Business Books.
3 Mitchell, A. (2001) 'The Emperor's new clothes: A backlash against branding?' *Market Leader*, Winter, 28–32.
4 Spector, R. (2001) *Amazon.com: Get Big Fast*, Random House Business Books.
5 Knobil, M. (editor-in-chief) (2001) *Superbrands*, Superbrands Ltd.
6 Pringle, H. and Gordon, W. (2001) *Brand Manners*, John Wiley.
7 Broadbent, T. (ed.) (2000) *Advertising Works 11*, World Advertising Research Center.

Chapter 3

1 Feldwick, P. (ed.) (1991) *Advertising Works 6*, NTC Publications.
2 Wetlaufer, S. (2001) 'The perfect paradox of star brands', *Harvard Business Review*, October, 116–23.
3 *Evening Standard*, 17 September 2001, 29.

Chapter 4

1 Fitzgerald, N. (2001) 'Life and death in the world of brands', *Market Leader*, Autumn, 17–22.
2 *Challenges*, 6 September 2001, 80–83.

Chapter 5

1 Collins, James C. and Porras, Jerry I. (1998) *Built to Last*, Century.
2 Cohen, B. and Greenfield, J. (1997) *Double Dip: Lead with Your Values and Make Money, Too*, Simon and Schuster.
3 Hamel, G. and Prahalad, C.K. (1996) *Competing for the Future*, Harvard Business School Press.
4 Starbucks website.

Chapter 6

1   *Guardian*, 18 August 2001, 34.
2   Lury, G. (1998) *Brandwatching*, Blackhall.

Chapter 7

1   Robinson, M. (2000) *100 Greatest TV Ads*, HarperCollins.
2   Kendall, N. (ed.) (1999) *Advertising Works 10*, NTC Publications.
3   Keller, K.L. (1998) *Strategic Brand Management*, Prentice-Hall.
4   Broadbent, T. (ed.) (2000) *Advertising Works 11*, World Advertising Research Center.

Chapter 8

1   Simms, J. (1999) 'Stretching core values', *Marketing*, 19 October, 49–50.
2   Symonds, W.C. (1999) '"Build a better mousetrap" is no claptrap'. *Business Week*, 1 February, 49.
3   Ball, J. (2000) 'Too cool for Chrysler?' *Wall Street Journal*, 21–22 July, 25.
4   Simms, J. (2001) 'When brands bounce back', *Marketing*, 15 February, 26–27.

Chapter 9

1   Taylor, D. (1999) *The Drivers of Brand Growth: Research Findings and Conclusions*, Added Value research paper.
2   Elgin, R. (2002) 'Happy workers keep the profits growing', *Sunday Times*, 10 March, Section 7, 5.
3   Trout, J. (2001) *Big Brand, Big Trouble: Lessons Learned the Hard Way*, John Wiley.
4   Kirby, J. (2001) 'Reinvention with respect: An interview with Jim Kelly of UPS', *Harvard Business Review*, November, 116–23.

Index